THE EASTERN &
NORTH EASTERN
THEN & NOW

GAVIN MORRISON

IAN ALLAN
Publishing

Contents

First published 1997

ISBN 0 7110 2529 0

All rights reserved. No part of this book may be reproduced or transmitted in any form or by any means, electronic or mechanical, including photocopying, recording or by any information storage and retrieval system, without permission from the Publisher in writing.

© Ian Allan Ltd 1997

Published by Ian Allan Publishing

an imprint of Ian Allan Ltd, Terminal House, Station Approach, Shepperton, Surrey TW17 8AS. Printed by Ian Allan Printing Ltd, at its works at Coombelands in Runneymede, England.

Code 9708/A

Bibliography

Clinker's Register of Closed Passenger Stations 1830-1980; C. R. Clinker; Avon Anglia
A-Z of Rail Reopenings; Railway Development Society
LNER locomotives; Railway Correspondence & Travel Society; various volumes
Railways in East Yorkshire; M. Bairstow; M. Bairstow
The Sheffield, Ashton under Lyne & Manchester Railway; M. Bairstow; M. Bairstow
The Pilmoor, Boroughbridge & Knaresborough Railway; P. Howet; M. Bairstow
Railways Around Harrogate; M. Bairstow & D. Beeken; M. Bairstow
Railways Around Whitby; M. Bairstow; M. Bairstow
Railways Through Airedale and Wharfedale; M. Bairstow; M. Bairstow
Past & Present 14: Cleveland & North Yorkshire; A. R. Thompson & K. Groundwater; Silver Link
Past & Present 12: East Anglia; D. Saunders & R. Adderson; Silver Link
Regional History of Britain's Railways; David & Charles; various volumes
The Age of the Electric Train; J. C. Gillham; Ian Allan Ltd
Passengers No More; G. Daniels & L. A. Dench; Ian Allan Ltd

Introduction

I was delighted to be offered the opportunity by Ian Allan Ltd to produce another volume in the 'Then & Now' series. This is the fourth volume and covers the lines of the London & North Eastern Railway in England. My travels have taken me as far north as Coldstream and as far south as New Barnet and, of course, all the way up the East Coast. My friends Brian Morrison and Ken Brunt sorted out the centre of London, where my route knowledge is limited. Having kept accurate records of the mileage involved in the two projects, it is interesting to see that the LMS totalled around 8,000 miles, of which I covered personally 6,700, and the LNER has taken about 6,500 in total.

It was just two years ago that I was writing the introduction for the LMR volume and, on reflection, the way that this project has been handled has been very similar to the earlier book. Again the pictures that have been used for the 'Then' shots have almost entirely come from the extensive Ian Allan Library and from my own collection. I have deliberately tried not to have too many of the very well-known locations in the big cities, although these have been covered, but rather to include the secondary, branch and minor lines, many of which have virtually completely vanished.

I have been taking railway pictures for around 40 years, and when one gets involved with a project such as this, one is continually asking oneself why I didn't visit these locations when the railways existed, rather than spending so much time at places like York and Doncaster, but I suppose I am no different from many other enthusiasts in that, in our younger days, most of us went to places where there were plenty of trains with the glamorous Pacifics, of which the LNER had more than its fair share.

I hope that I have got the number of pictures for each of the constituent companies in about the same ratio as the track miles that each of them operated. The northeast seems to have come out well on top in terms of the number of photographs, no doubt in part because I have more 'Then' pictures in this area than the others, but there was a very dense concentration of lines in this area, every valley into the hills having a line, and many of these going over the hills.

As before, with only some 300 locations to cover such a vast area, there will be obvious omissions. It is odd that in such a large collection as the Ian Allan Library that it proved impossible to track down photographs of places like Scunthorpe and Barnetby, which is ironic considering that enthusiasts today flock to the latter to photograph the wide variety of locomotive-hauled freight trains (by today's standards) that run to Immingham.

Once again, without the help of many local people, and particularly the owners of some of the beautifully restored station houses, many of the 'Now' pictures would not have been possible. My grateful thanks go to these people who, without exception, assisted me in every way that they could. I visited an auction in East Anglia — although I didn't buy anything — in order to get permission to stand in the correct spot. I also visited several factories, the inevitable supermarket of course and more Station Roads that anybody else in the country other than the compilers of the volumes on the Great Western and Southern in this series.

As before it is very difficult to single out a particular location where the change have been more dramatic, although two do come to mind in Nottingham, one being the old Nottingham Victoria site where a vast new shop/office complex has been built very recently and the other is at New Basford where a massive infill operation has been undertaken, but there are many more. The Great Central as a line seems to have vanished beyond recognition, especially around the Nottingham area. The Hull & Barnsley is also disappearing completely in places. Fortunately fine stations like York, Darlington, Newcastle, Marylebone and King's Cross have altered little, other than for track rationalisation.

Where I have not been able to stand in the same position for a wide variety of reasons, I have tied to explain why in the captions. Occasionally I have used a wider angle lens to show more of the location than was the case in the 'Then' picture in order to give more interest. Do look very carefully at some of the comparisons; they are not always obvious. A reviewer of the LMR volume wrote of the pictures I used of my home town, Mirfield, that I had included the old shed in the 'Then' picture but not in the 'Now' shot. The truth is that trees had grown, completely obliterating the shed from view.

The vast majority of the 'Now' photographs taken in these volumes are ones which, under normal circumstances, one would never take, as they are full of things which enthusiasts now consider as unacceptable. This is perfectly true, and it was only when I went out to cover the locations around Leeds, some of which I had not visited for 10 or more years, that I realised why one seldom sees pictures taken in Leeds these days other that at the station. All the good and well-used locations, once used by fine photographers like Bishop Treacy and Kenneth Field to name but two, are now history. Wortley Junction, Leeds Central, Copley Hill, Beeston Junction, Marsh Lane to name but a few have all suffered, and I suppose that it is the same in other big cities. This probably helps to explain why more and more photographers seem to congregate in the same places these days. I know there are other reasons, not least of which is where locomotive-hauled trains can still be encountered, but I do wonder whether or not there are more people taking photographs now than in the 1950s and 1960s.

Again I must extend my thanks to the many people who have helped with the book: to Brian Morrison and Ken Brunt for helping me with the pictures for the centre of London; to Peter Waller of Ian Allan Ltd for assistance with certain dates and other information; and, finally, to my navigator Keith Marshall, without whom the book would have taken much longer. He surprised not me, but also himself, when he managed to get me to Brinkburn station on the Rothbury line without taking a wrong turning.

I have tried in this volume to include as many opening and closing dates as possible, along with brief information on some of the locomotives that appear in the 'Then' shots.

Projects such as these tend to portray all doom and gloom on the railways, which has certainly been the case over the last few decades, but after all the uncertainties of the last few years, it is good to be able to report in the captions about the reopening of stations and the reopening of a line (that to Redmire). The next few years should be very interesting, so I hope that you enjoy looking back at the past and comparing it with the present, but also continue to take an interest in Britain's railways in the future.

Gavin Morrison,
Mirfield,
March 1997

Great Central Railway

Although the Great Central Railway was the last of the major railway companies to rise to prominence, through the completion of its London Extension in 1898/99, its origins lay much earlier in the history of Britain's railways. The act permitting construction of the London Extension from Annesley (north of Nottingham) to Quainton Road (where it met up with the Metropolitan Railway) — was passed on 28 March 1893. The act was under the name of the Manchester, Sheffield & Lincolnshire Railway; the name Great Central Railway. was not adopted until 1 August 1897.

The MS&LR was created through the merger of the Great Grimsby & Sheffield Junction, the Sheffield, Ashton-under-Lyne & Manchester and the Sheffield & Lincolnshire Junction railways. Although the merger commenced on 1 January 1847, the three companies retained their separate identities until August 1849. The GG&SJR dated from 1845 and it was promoted with the intention of constructing a network of lines in the north Lincolnshire area. The first section, from New Holland to Grimsby, opened on 1 March 1848. This was followed by the sections from Ulceby to Brigg and Barnetby to Market Raisen on 1 November 1848. The latter line was extended to Lincoln on 18 December 1848. The Barton-on-Humber branch followed on 1 March 1849. The line from Brigg to Gainsborough opened on 2 April 1850 and thence to Woodhouse Junction (via Retford) on 16 July 1850. The Lincoln-Retford line was opened on 7 August 1850. The extension of the line from Grimsby to Cleethorpes did not materialise until 6 April 1863.

The SA&MR was incorporated in May 1837 with the intention of building a railway running across the Pennines. The route selected was difficult and amongst engineering works undertaken was the Woodhead Tunnel; at the time this was the longest tunnel ever attempted. The line opened from Manchester to Woodhead on 8 August 1844 and from Dunford Bridge to Sheffield on 14 July 1845. The section through the tunnel was opened on 23 December 1845. Initially the Woodhead Tunnel was only a single bore, but a second bore was soon needed and this was opened in 1852,

The third constituent of the MS&LR was the Sheffield & Lincolnshire Junction Railway. This was promoted as a line linking Sheffield with the line towards Gainsborough. The route, through Beighton, was opened on 12 February 1849.

Other constituents of the GCR included the Lancashire, Derbyshire & East Coast Railway, which was promoted to link Manchester with the East Coast at Sutton-on-Sea. The only sections which opened were those from Chesterfield to Lincoln (8 March 1897) and a branch to Beighton (May 1900). It was incorporated in the GCR in 1907. The GCR also provided the LNER with its only toehold in Wales, through the Wrexham, Mold & Connah's Quay Railway, which was vested in the GCR in 1905; the first section of the line — from Buckley to the River Dee — opened in 1862.

The event which took the MS&LR from being purely a regional railway into one serving London was the completion of the last main line to the Metropolis. The transition from MS&LR to GCR has been recounted on many occasions; suffice to say here that the main line was opened formally on 9 March 1899. There were a number of post-1900 developments; these included the construction of the docks at Immingham along with the associated Grimsby & Immingham tramway, making the GCR one of the few railway companies to operate an electric tramway.

The history of Britain's railways post-Grouping and post-Nationalisation has not been kind to the GCR. Apart from the closure of the main line north of Aylesbury, much of the network serving the area south and east of Sheffield has also disappeared, as has the famous Woodhead route. Survivals include the line from Sheffield to Retford, Gainsborough and Cleethorpes, the line from Lincoln to Barnetby and the route from Barnetby to Doncaster, as well as the line from Wrexham to the Wirral peninsula. A section of the closed main line — from Loughborough to Leicester North — is preserved and there are plans to extend this northwards to the southern outskirts of Nottingham.

Marylebone

Then: 1 September 1966
Opened in 1899 as the last of the London main line terminals, the Great Central's station was at the southern point of a route that offered the potential for high-speed running north to the Midlands and Yorkshire. This role the GCR main line fulfilled well until Nationalisation, when it became increasingly clear that its services could be easily accommodated on other lines. Gradually the expresses were withdrawn. Shortly before the withdrawal of through services over the route, ex-LMS Class 5 No 45493, reflecting the change of regional ownership that had accelerated the line's demise, prepares to leave on the 2.38pm semi-fast service to Nottingham. Ex-LMS types dominated the passenger services in the last years, although DMUs, seen to the left of the Class 5, had taken over the local services to Aylesbury and other destinations. *John H. Bird*

Now: January 1997
Through services over the ex-GC main line ceased on 5 September 1966. Although the whole ambience of the station has changed since the advent of the Chiltern Turbos, this particular view has altered little.
Class 165/0 No 165032 awaits departure as the 14.15 service to Aylesbury via High Wycombe. It is worth remembering that not so long ago there was a question mark over whether Marylebone would survive or not. *Brian Morrison*

Rickmansworth

Then: 15 June 1962
Situated on the Metropolitan & Great Central Joint line, railway services first reached Rickmansworth on 1 September 1887 with the opening of the line north from Pinner. The line was extended northwards to Chalfont and Chesham on 8 July 1889. Back in 1962, the Aylesbury-Marylebone services were in the hands of Fairburn 2-6-4Ts, these having replaced the 'L1' class 2-6-4Ts. On this occasion No 42157 is shown arriving on the 5.48pm service from Marylebone. *L. Sandler*

Now: 22 September 1996
Little seems to have altered over the years with the layout of the track at the station remaining similar, although some of the buildings in the background seem to have vanished. The services to Aylesbury are now operated by Chiltern Railways' Turbo trains. *Author*

Chesham

Then: 25 December 1953
The Chesham branch opened on 8 July 1889. For a period it was the terminus of the line northwards; however, on 1 September 1892 the line north from Chalfont to Aylesbury was opened and Chesham was relegated to a branch status. In 1941 auto-trains were introduced on the branch and three Class C13 4-4-2Ts were modified for this service. These were Nos 7418, 7420 and 7438. One of the trio, now No 67418, is shown ready to depart for Chalfont & Latimer with the 12.14pm service. *N. W. Spinks*

Amersham

Then: 26 May 1963
This was one of the more important intermediate stations on the Metropolitan and Great Central Joint. On 26 May 1963 a special train was run to commemorate the centenary of the opening of the first section of the Metropolitan Railway, a tour which took the train as far north as Aylesbury. It was hauled over the Met & GC Joint line by 'Jubilee' No 45709 *Implacable*. The locomotive was based at Saltley (Birmingham) and had hauled the train tender-first north to Aylesbury. *Alec Swain*

Now: 20 September 1996
The station has changed little over the years, although it is now well painted and the booking hall area has been modernised. Class 165 Turbo No 165034 is shown arriving with the 15.30 departure to Marylebone. *Author*

Aylesbury

Then: 23 June 1958
One of the main stations on the Met & GC Joint line, Aylesbury was also the junction for the GW & GC Joint line via Little Kimble to Princes Risborough. Here the 7.20pm service from Quainton Road to Marylebone prepares to leave headed by Neasden-allocated Class L1 2-6-4T No 67767. *M. Mitchell*

Now: 22 September 1996
London Transport took over sole operation of the line in 1960 with electrification and services now form part of the Metropolitan. This view, taken from the platform rather than the track, shows that most of the features present in 1953 are still around. The station is kept in immaculate condition and is a credit to all involved. *Author*

Now: 18 September 1996
Passenger services north of Aylesbury were withdrawn on 5 September 1966, but the station is still served by passenger services over both the Met & GC and GW & GC routes from the south (although Metropolitan trains no longer operate over the route beyond Amersham). Freight facilities were withdrawn in December 1974, leaving the town with a strong commuter-based passenger service. Aylesbury station has been modernised, as have the other Chiltern line stations. The modern Class 165 No 165009 has just arrived at 17.10 from Marylebone and is shown against the background of the refurbished station. *Author*

Quainton Road

Then: 1935
This pre-World War 2 photograph shows the lines leading down the branch to Brill, which lost its services on 2 December 1935. Quainton Road was the northernmost point of the Met & GC Joint line as part of the GC main line; from here northwards the main line was under the sole control of the GCR, whilst the Met & GC Joint headed northeastwards to meet up with the LNWR at Verney Junction. The branch to Brill had opened in 1872. *Ian Allan Library (L&GRP 7765)*

Although passenger traffic over the ex-GC main line was withdrawn in 1966, the line north from Aylesbury via Quainton Road to Calvert (thence by a spur linked into the ex-LNWR Oxford-Cambridge line) remains operational to serve the waste disposal terminal at Akeman Street; the routes to both Verney Junction and Brill are closed. The rest of the extensive site is now used by the Buckinghamshire Railway Centre, which first opened to the public in 1969. The centre has sidings located either side of (but separate from) the Railtrack route. As can be seen, the centre has built a repair shed on the site of the erstwhile Brill branch. This houses some of the large collection of rolling stock. Illustrated is one of the centre's many ex-industrial locomotives, Bagnall 0-4-0T *Swanscombe* of 1891. *Author*

Brackley Central

Then: 2 September 1966
Brackley Central opened with the rest of the Great Central's London Extension in 1898/99. Stanier Class 5 No 44872 calls with a Nottingham-Neasden parcels service on 2 September 1966, one day before closure of the line. The vans had travelled north the night before laden with newspapers. Goods services had ceased on 14 June 1965.
J. M. French

Now: 18 September 1996
The site is now half occupied by a factory, which is behind where I took this photograph. The actual station buildings, which were situated at a higher (road) level, still survive, but are now used as offices for an ATS tyre centre. *Author*

Beaconsfield

Then: 16 September 1958
Situated on the Great Western & Great Central Joint line from High Wycombe, passenger services were introduced in 1906. Leicester-allocated Class V2 2-6-2 No 60842 approaches the station at the head of a midday train to Manchester London Road. Most of the Great Central expresses used the alternative route northwards via Amersham. *Author*

Woodford Halse

Then: 29 August 1959
The railway first arrived here in 1898, and it developed into an important centre on the Great Central. Most freight used to change locomotives here, and in 1950 the shed (coded 38E) had an allocation of 54 locomotives, which included 10 Gresley Class V2s as well as four Class B17 'Sandringhams'. The 'Austerity' 2-8-0s were the main freight locomotives at that time, but the line later became synonymous with the Class 9F 2-10-0s. The shed code changed to 2G in 1958 (on the transfer to LMR control), then to 2F, and then to 1G between 1963 and 1965 when it closed. By the date of closure, all locomotives allocated were ex-LMS. A Nottingham-Marylebone train is shown leaving, headed by Class B1 4-6-0 No 61206. The station can be seen just north of the junction with the spur from the Stratford-upon-Avon & Midland Junction Railway. *S. Creer*

Charwelton

Then: 13 July 1959
Annesley-based Class 9F No 92090 heads a down freight just north of the station. *Author*

Now: 20 September 1996
The bushes on the embankment have undoubtedly taken over in the last 38 years. The track has been rationalised and it is certainly impossible to travel direct to Manchester over the route now. Class 165 Turbo unit No 165017 approaches with the 14.44 arrival from Marylebone. As elsewhere, this route now sees very little in the way of locomotive-hauled trains. *Author*

Now: 18 September 1996
Through services over the Great Central were withdrawn on 5 September 1966 and at the same time the section between Claydon and Rugby Central closed completely. At the same time all services were withdrawn on the ex-GCR line from Woodford Halse to Banbury. Now that the railways have long gone, this Northamptonshire village has become a quiet country community, although the presence of the railway can still be seen beside the houses in the area of the station. A local farmer's sheds now stand on the ex-GCR trackbed. *Author*

Now: 18 September 1996
The station closed on 4 March 1963. The section between Rugby Central and Calvert was closed completely with the withdrawal of through passenger services over the ex-GC main line on 5 September 1966. Almost exactly 30 years after the area saw its last train, the trackbed and shallow embankments are gradually being overgrown by trees and bushes. *Author*

Charwelton (looking north)

Then: 6 May 1961
This picture of Class B1 4-6-0 No 61154 heading an up Cup Final special from Leicester to Wembley clearly shows the southern entrance to Cadeby Tunnel, which was 1 mile 1,240yd long. Construction of the tunnel took from 1893 to 1897, the line opening for freight on 25 July 1898 and to passenger services on 15 March 1899. *L. W. Roy*

Lutterworth

Then: 13 July 1959
One of the famous 'windcutter' coal trains, headed by an Annesley-based Class 9F 2-10-0 No 92074 makes speedy progress south as it approaches Lutterworth, between Leicester and Rugby. *Author*

Now: 18 September 1996
The tops of the bridge over the railway can still be seen in Gilmarton Road, Lutterworth, but I found it very difficult to establish exactly where I had taken the picture in 1959. Behind the trees is an industrial estate and, hidden by them on the right, the M1 motorway. Obviously, when the motorway was built there were big earth movements, which increased the difficulty in trying to sort out the land layout. *Author*

Now: 18 September 1996
The trackbed of this location is still relatively free of trees and bushes, although the tunnel entrance is now obscured. The ventilation shaft is still clearly visible. *Author*

Rugby Central

Then: 2 April 1963
This typical Great Central island platform station opened with the rest of the London Extension in 1898 for freight and 1899 for passenger services. Looking in ex-works condition, Class 9F 2-10-0 No 92076 passes with an up freight from Annesley to Woodford Halse. *D. Smith*

Now: 18 September 1996
Following the cessation of through passenger services over the route in 1966, Rugby Central became the southern terminus of a local service northwards to Nottingham. This was withdrawn on 5 May 1969. As can be seen behind the bushes, the platform still exists, but the site has returned to nature and is now part of the Great Central Walkway. It was being well used by people taking their dogs for a walk when I visited the site. *Author*

Ashby Magna

Then: 9 May 1966

This was one of three intermediate stations between Rugby Central and Leicester Central. Freight services were first run over the line in 1898 and passenger services the following year. It was located on the seven-mile gradient of 1 in 176 between mileposts 92 and 99, and northbound trains frequently reached speeds in the upper 80s, and even occasionally over 90mph on this stretch. About four months prior to the withdrawal of through services, Class 5 No 45288 — reflecting the fact that the line had passed to LMR control — departs with the 6.15pm Nottingham Victoria-Rugby Central service. On the right can be seen the M1 motorway.
M. Mitchell

Now: 18 October 1996

Through services over the ex-GC main line were withdrawn on 5 September 1966 and the last local services over the Rugby-Nottingham section followed on 5 May 1969. Today the station yard is occupied by a timber company. The road overbridge has been filled in, but the top is still visible. As can be seen, the trees and bushes have grown to a great height, blocking out the view and the noise of the M1 to some extent — no doubt to the relief of the owner of the timber company. *Author*

Quorn & Woodhouse

Then: 24 July 1961

The station here was, like that at Belgrave & Birstall, the product of the GC's London Extension, although the facilities provided were more significant. Standard Class 5MT No 73156 arrives at the station with the 9.30am local from Leicester Central to Nottingham Victoria. This locomotive is now awaiting restoration on the East Lancs Railway. *M. Mitchell*

Belgrave & Birstall

Then: 24 July 1961
It was during 1898 that the Great Central opened the section of track between Annesley and Quainton Road to freight traffic; passenger traffic was introduced the following year. This station was situated about two miles north of Leicester Central and comprised a single island platform with no freight facilities. Class B1 4-6-0 No 61187, in dirty external condition, hurries through the station with the 8.40pm Nottingham Victoria-Marylebone service. *M. Mitchell*

Now: 27 October 1996
Through passenger services over the ex-GC main line were withdrawn in September 1966, although Belgrave & Birstall station had already lost its passenger services by that date, being closed on 4 March 1963. Local services over the Rugby Central-Nottingham Arkwright Street section were withdrawn on 5 May 1969. Although the original preservation plans were ambitious, a base was established by the new Great Central at Loughborough and since closure much has been achieved. The track at Belgrave & Birstall was lifted and the original station buildings were demolished in 1977. In 1991 a new station, named Leicester North, was opened some 300yd south of the original station. This is the terminus of the preserved line which will, if all plans come to fruition, eventually reach as far as Ruddington on the southern outskirts of Nottingham. *Author*

Now: 27 October 1996
Like Belgrave & Birstall, Quorn & Woodhouse lost its passenger services on 4 March 1963, some time before the actual closure of the route. Happily the station is now part of the preserved Great Central and, unlike Leicester North, the original building still survives; in fact, very little has changed, which is a great credit to the preservation company. Here Class 9F 2-10-0 No 92203 leaves for Leicester. This type of locomotive was frequently seen on the line, covering both passenger and freight duties. They are particularly well remembered for their duties on the famous 'windcutter' freight turns to Woodford Halse. *Author*

Nottingham Victoria

Then: 7 August 1965
This impressive station was opened on 24 May 1900, without any public ceremony. Over the years it was the location of some excellent photographs, especially at the north end where there was the entrance to Mansfield Road Tunnel. The station was jointly owned by the GC and GN railways. LMS Class 5 No 45299 is pictured ready to leave with the 8.15am service to Marylebone. *J. Cupit*

Now: 12 October 1966
Through services over the ex-GC main line from Marylebone to Sheffield Victoria were withdrawn on 5 September 1966. For the next year, Nottingham Victoria was the northernmost terminus for a local service running south to Rugby, but on 4 September 1967 these were curtailed to Nottingham Arkwright Street and Victoria closed. The changes to the station site have been dramatic. I cannot guarantee to be standing in exactly the same position as the 'Then' shot, but I cannot be far out. The small car park was about the only open space in the immediate area. Little remains to show that a railway ever existed, although to the south some of the viaduct arches still exist and I believe the tunnel entrance still remains behind the buildings illustrated. *Author*

New Basford

Then: Undated
This undated photograph, taken probably not long before closure of the line, shows Stanier Class 8F 2-8-0 No 48432 drifting down the 1 in 132 gradient towards Mansfield Road Tunnel on the north side of Nottingham Victoria station. The typical Great Central island platform station can be seen to the left of the signalbox. *J. Cupit*

Now: 29 November 1996
I could hardly believe my eyes when I got to this location. The deep cutting has been completely filled in and levelled to provide what appeared to be a rather ill-kept football pitch. Houses have also been built on the station area. I find this one of the most dramatic comparisons in the book. The line was closed to passenger services with the withdrawal of through Sheffield-Marylebone trains in September 1966. *Author*

Kirkby Bentinck

Then: 22 August 1959
The line here opened on 24 October 1892 when MS&LR services were extended from Staveley Town to Annesley Junction. The station was just over the summit of the long climb from Bulwell Common at 1 in 130, about one mile north of Annesley Tunnel. An extremely dirty Class B1 4-6-0 No 61381 is caught passing the station at the head of a summer Saturdays Only 8.10am Swansea-York service.
P. J. Shoesmith

Shirebrook North

Then: July 1954
This small town could once boast three railways stations — North, South and West — owned by the Great Central, the Great Northern and the Midland respectively. The GCR arrived here on 8 March 1897 with the opening of the Chesterfield-Lincoln line and the branch towards Sheffield. From 1897 until 1924 the station was known as Langwith Junction. Judging by the number of passengers on the platform, the occasion of this photograph would appear to be a rail tour. The line from Shirebrook North to Sheffield lost its passenger services on 10 September 1939. Shirebrook North was also the junction of the GNR line north from Nottingham, which opened in 1901. This line lost its passenger services on 14 September 1931.
Ian Allan Library (K2302)

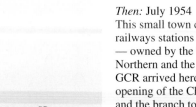

Shirebrook Junction

Then: Whit Monday 1964
The immediate area around Shirebrook was served by the Great Central, Great Northern and Midland railways. The first railway through the town was the Midland's which opened in 1875. This view shows the Midland line heading left to right, with the link to the ex-Great Central line heading towards the camera. Ex-LMS Class 5 4-6-0 No 45253 is caught at the head of an excursion train from Nottingham to Skegness. The ex-Midland station, which became known as Shirebrook West in 1951, is located behind the bridge on the left; it was to close on 12 October 1964
J. S. Hancock

Now: 29 November 1996
All services ceased here on 4 March 1963 (although the line remained open until the withdrawal of through services between Sheffield and Marylebone in September 1966). Sections of the old GC main line around Nottinghamshire are sometimes difficult to trace. Nothing at this location remains to show that the railway once passed this spot, the link between the two pictures being the house on the right-hand side. Behind where I took the photograph are traces of the goods yard, where the shed is still in use by a haulage contractor. *Author*

Now: 11 August 1996
The line from Chesterfield to Shirebrook North lost its passenger services on 3 December 1951 (at which time the line between Markham Junction and Shirebrook closed completely) and those from Shirebrook North to Lincoln were withdrawn on 19 September 1955. Freight services continued until 1965. The area once occupied by the station is currently undeveloped and derelict. Traces of the station platform can still be seen in the undergrowth. The ex-GCR line is open to the east of Shirebrook as far as the power station at High Marnham. *Author*

Now: 12 October 1996
Little has changed over 32 years between these two photographs, except that the trees have grown. There is now a triangle at Shirebrook, with a link between the ex-GC route and the ex-Midland line to the north. There is a considerable amount of merry-go-round traffic over these lines. The diesel depot is alongside the now-closed station on the left, but this has recently been taken out of use. There is talk of the station being reopened when the 'Robin Hood' line from Nottingham is extended to Worksop. Unfortunately, there were no trains due when I visited the location on this Saturday. *Author*

Woodhouse

Then: 8 June 1960

Situated five miles south of Sheffield Victoria on the ex-Great Central main line southeastwards towards Retford. It opened from Sheffield to Woodhouse Junction on 12 February 1849 and thence to Gainsborough on 17 July the same year. The station was originally sited at Woodhouse Junction, but was relocated to its current position in October 1875. Woodhouse Junction was the location of a freight-only branch that served Birley Colliery; it opened in June 1855 and closed shortly after Nationalisation. The junction with the main line south to Nottingham and London was just to the east of Woodhouse. 'Britannia' Pacific No 70038 *Robin Hood* passes the station non-stop on the Liverpool-Harwich boat train service, which departed from Sheffield Victoria at 3.30pm having travelled over the Woodhead route. Woodhouse was the eastern extremity of the 1,500V dc electrification scheme on this route out of Sheffield and the overhead masts can be seen behind the end of the train.
G. Newall

Sheffield Victoria

Then: 18 April 1956

The station opened to traffic on 15 September 1851, long before it became associated with the Great Central main line. This superb picture taken in 1956, two years after the opening throughout of the electrification to Manchester, shows Wakefield-allocated Class 5 No 45101 having just arrived with the Bradford portion of the 'South Yorkshireman'. This locomotive worked the first 'South Yorkshireman' when the train was introduced in May 1948. In the centre road are additional coaches, which will be attached to the train for its journey to Marylebone. This rake is headed by one of the Gresley 'A1' Pacifics built prior to the Grouping in 1923. It was rebuilt as an 'A3' in 1942, becoming No 60102 *Sir Frederick Banbury* in 1948. It was allocated to the GC line from 1949 until 1957, when it returned to its old haunts at King's Cross.
R. Hewitt

Staveley

Then: 9 May 1964
This picture was not taken on the Great Central main line, but on a line alongside the former shed (which closed in 1965). The shed here was originally coded 38D in 1948, but became 41H in July 1958. The main line is seen in the background at a higher level to the left of Class O4/8 2-8-0 No 63914, which was at the head of some coal wagons. The ex-GCR station was called Staveley Town and was the junction between the main line and the Chesterfield loop. The station lost its passenger services on 4 March 1963, but through services continued to use the main line until their withdrawal in September 1966. *Author*

Now: 12 October 1996
The ex-GCR main line south of Sheffield to Arkwright remained open from Beighton Station Junction to Staveley until 23 August 1982 when a new spur to the ex-Midland route at Staveley allowed traffic from Arkwright Colliery to be diverted. The colliery at Arkwright was to close in 1988. Since closure of the shed and line, the location has altered dramatically. The ground has been landscaped and new houses built to the right of the photograph, with the road shown running along the back of the houses. *Author*

Now: 12 October 1996
The electrification masts and sidings have long gone, and the station is unstaffed and boarded up. The only regular trains using the line are the Sheffield-Retford-Lincoln trains, Pacer No 142094 forming the 09.46 from Sheffield to Retford. The line is also used when engineering diversions are needed around Sheffield. *Author*

Now: 11 February 1997
Sheffield Victoria closed on 5 January 1970 with the withdrawal of passenger services on the Woodhead route. It retained a ghostly afterlife, however, as it was passed by trains on the Sheffield-Huddersfield route, which continued to use the line to Penistone and to reverse at Nunnery Junction until 16 May 1983 when these services were diverted to run via Barnsley. The station became derelict, but the site has now been cleared and part is now occupied by a new Holiday Inn Hotel which is linked to the old Victoria Hotel to the left. A single track, used for freight only to Deepcar, still passes the site. *Author*

Retford (Whisker Hill Junction)

Then: Undated
The Manchester, Sheffield & Lincolnshire Railway line between
Sheffield and Gainsborough opened on 16 July 1849. This junction is
situated to the west of the town and is the point where the link to the
East Coast main line joins the route. Pictured is Class B1 No 61150
rounding the sharp curve at the junction, with a Cleethorpes-Sheffield
stopping train which had called at the ex-GNR station. As can be seen,
there were quite extensive yards at this point, before the ex-MS&LR line
converged into two lines to cross the GNR main line on the level to the
south of Retford station. *A. M. Ross*

Now: 11 February 1997
There have been a lot of changes over the years. The junction is now
about half-a-mile behind where I was standing and Class 153
No 153352 is about to cross the old GCR line on a new bridge installed
when the 'fly-under' was built. This meant that trains on the old GC
route no longer had access to Retford station from the east, with the
result that new platforms were built on the lower level for these services.
The train illustrated is the 10.53 from Retford to Sheffield; trains
connect with services over the ECML that call at Retford. The cutting
created by the work of the 1960s can be clearly seen on the right of the
picture. *Author*

Mexborough

Then: 1 July 1963
Ultimately this location became a busy centre for the GCR, with a large locomotive shed providing power for the considerable amount of freight traffic in the area. The line from Doncaster South Junction to Swinton, through Mexborough, was opened under the aegis of the South Yorkshire Railway on 10 July 1849. The station at Mexborough itself was resited to its present location in April 1871. A westbound freight, headed by 'Austerity' 2-8-0 No 90330, passes through the station.
G. T. Robinson

Now: 11 October 1996
The main station buildings still exist, and are extremely well looked after by the staff. A frequent service of Pacers and Sprinters operates the busy Sheffield-Doncaster route. In addition Cross Country 125s and a few freights still use the route. One of the West Yorkshire PTE Class 141s, No 141115, enters the station on the 13.25 to Sheffield.
Author

Conisbrough

Then: 20 November 1966
The section of the surviving Sheffield-Doncaster route from
Mexborough East Junction to Doncaster eventually became part of the
GCR. It provided one of the main access routes for coal traffic from the
Yorkshire coalfield to the east coast. Conisbrough, perhaps more
famous for its castle, is situated about seven miles west of Doncaster.
On this occasion unusual motive power, in the form of Southern Region
'Merchant Navy' Pacific No 35026 *Lamport & Holt Line*, passes with a
special. At this time it was the first occasion that a 'Merchant Navy' had
traversed the route. In 1966 the Doncaster platforms were an island and
there were also a few sidings. *Author*

Now: 11 October 1996
Today the station is still open and is used by the frequent Doncaster-
Sheffield trains. There are now only two platforms in use and the station
is unstaffed. The former station house is, however, occupied. Sprinter
No 156489 calls at the station with the 14.00 service to Sheffield. As
can be seen, the trees have grown considerably. *Author*

Wath on Dearne/Manvers

Then: 25 March 1977

This is a scene on the former Great Central route out of the once busy Wath Yard, which was the terminus of the electrified line across the Pennines to Manchester via Woodhead. The line from Mexborough to Barnsley was opened to freight traffic in 1850/51 and to passenger traffic on 1 July 1851. By the date of this photograph, passenger traffic had ceased (on 5 January 1970). Class 37 No 37111 is seen heading a train of lifted track towards Mexborough. It has just passed under the former Midland main line, which headed north from Rotherham through the famous Manvers coking plant. The route towards York headed east from the junction visible.
Author

Now: 11 October 1996

This is one of the most dramatic comparisons in the book. Passenger services over the ex-Midland main line were withdrawn officially on 12 May 1986 and the line has been cut back so that it now terminates, as a freight-only line, at Houghton Main Colliery to the north of Bolton on Dearne. The line closed completely between Wath Road Junction at Houghton Main on 1 June 1987. The ex-GCR lines in the area gradually closed following the withdrawal of the electric services over the Woodhead route in 1981 and the demise of the coal industry in the district. The section illustrated here closed completely in 1988. By October 1996 the track had been lifted — having been reduced from four to two tracks prior to closure — and the trackbed would appear to be under redevelopment as a road. All signs of the Manvers coking plant have disappeared, as have traces of almost all the traditional industries. A modern industrial estate, 'Manvers', has been laid out in the background on the right-hand side. The surviving lines visible on the rail overbridge carry the line towards Bolton on Dearne.
Author

Penistone

Then: 27 June 1964
This expanding town is situated high in the Pennines. Railway services first arrived with the opening of the line from Dunford Bridge to Sheffield on 14 July 1845. The town became a junction in 1854 with the opening of the line towards Barnsley and the final link came with the opening of the line north towards Huddersfield (operated by the Lancashire & Yorkshire) that opened in 1874. As a result, Penistone developed into a busy railway centre. On 27 June 1964 a Railway Correspondence & Travel Society special is show passing *en route* to Woodhead headed by electric locomotive No 26000 *Tommy* and 'B1' No 61372. *Author*

Silkstone

Then: 9 May 1959
Heading east from Penistone, there were three stations before Barnsley was reached. The first of these was Silkstone, which was located just after the junction for the Worsbrough route. Services were inaugurated on 1 July 1854. Here Class C14 4-4-2T No 67445 was in charge of the local Doncaster-Penistone service. *Author*

Now: 13 September 1996
Silkstone lost its passenger services on 27 June 1959 with the withdrawal of the Doncaster-Penistone service. Complete withdrawal of passenger services over the route occurred on 5 January 1970. However, as part of a scheme to retain the Sheffield-Huddersfield service, passenger trains were reinstated in 1983 and the station here was reopened on 26 November 1984. As can be seen, the track has been singled and the platform cut back. West Yorkshire PTE Class 144 No 144019 enters the station on the 12.06 service to Barnsley and Sheffield. The line seldom sees a locomotive-hauled train, except for the occasional enthusiasts' special or specials run on behalf of the Green Party, which have over the past few years sometimes started or called at Penistone. *Author*

Now: 13 September 1996
Today, following the withdrawal of freight services over the Woodhead route (in 1981) and the transfer of the Huddersfield-Sheffield service via Barnsley in 1983, the railway presence at Penistone is much reduced. The surviving routes are those that arrived last, the original main line from Manchester to Sheffield having now been completely lifted. Most of the old railway trackbed is now derelict, and the only action is the hourly service over the Huddersfield-Barnsley-Sheffield route. However, the tall signalbox survives, although this is due to be taken out of use in 1997. *Author*

Dodworth

Then: 2 July 1966
This was the second of the three intermediate stations on the line between Penistone and Barnsley. It opened on 1 July 1854. During the 1960s the Bradford-Poole summer Saturdays only service was routed over the line and here Farnley Junction-allocated 'Jubilee' No 45647 *Sturdee* storms up the gradient towards Penistone with the train for Bradford. The line to the left went to the local colliery. *Author*

Now: 13 September 1996
Passenger services over the route were withdrawn on 5 January 1970 contemporary with the cessation of services over the Woodhead route, although Dodworth station itself closed on 29 June 1959. However, the threatened closure of the Huddersfield-Sheffield service (with its inconvenient reversal in Sheffield) led to a reappraisal of the rail routes in the district and the reintroduction of passenger services over the Penistone-Barnsley line in 1983. As can be seen, the line has been singled, but the signalbox still controls the level crossing, although it is due to be taken out of service during 1997. The old footbridge, from which the 'Then' photograph was taken, has been removed, so the picture of Class 144 unit No 144013 on the 12.24 service to Huddersfield had to be taken from track level. The route now enjoys an hourly service. *Author*

Immingham Docks

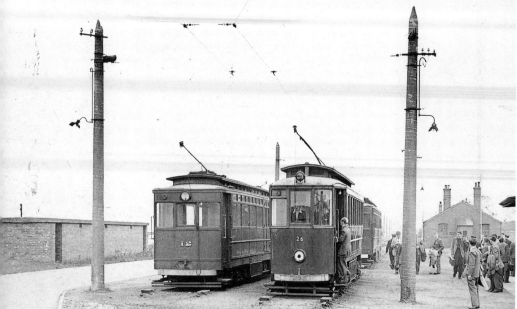

Then: 21 June 1953
The Grimsby & Immingham tramway, built by the GCR, was primarily to convey the dock workers from Grimsby to Immingham, and staff to the locomotive shed. It opened on 15 May 1912 and had no connection with the main line. This picture was taken at Immingham Docks and shows two different types of cars. No 12 on the left was built by Brush in 1913 and seated 64; it was withdrawn in July 1961. On the right is No 26, which was an ex-Gateshead car. It was built at Gateshead in 1925 and entered service on the Grimsby & Immingham in February 1952. No 26 was also withdrawn in July 1961, along with 24 other trams, when services ceased on 1 July that year.
A. A. Jackson

Grimsby Town

Then: 13 October 1956
The first train to reach Grimsby, operated under the aegis of the Manchester, Sheffield & Lincolnshire Railway, did so on 29 February 1848. At the time both the MS&LR line and the Great Northern's route to Louth were both nearing completing, and both opened to the public during March the same year. The station at Grimsby was used by services operated by both the GC and GN railways. Here the 12.15pm train to King's Cross (via Boston) is standing in the up platform headed by 'B1' class 4-6-0 No 61205. *R. E. Vincent*

New Clee (Cleethorpes)

Then: 26 August 1959
Carlisle Kingmoor-based Class 5 4-6-0
No 44792 approaches Cleethorpes with an
excursion. *John Willerton*

Now: 18 February 1995
The changes here have been dramatic, with
the running lines reduced to a single track
and the sidings all lifted. Class 47/7
No 47739 *Resourceful* makes a welcome
change from the usual Sprinter or Pacer
over the route as its approaches Cleethorpes
with a Pathfinder special; later the same day
the special visited both Grimsby and
Immingham Docks. At the rear of the train
is Class 56 No 56039 *Port of Hull. Author*

Now: 9 November 1996
The staff in the security office in the docks
had no difficulty in directing me to where
the terminus used to be. The trams are now
replaced by a Stagecoach-owned double-
deck bus, which was going to Cleethorpes.
Author

Now: 9 November 1996
The 'Then' photograph was taken from the
Garden Street signalbox at the east end of
the station. This structure still stands, but is
now unused and the staircase to it has been
blocked. As a result, the 'Now' photograph
had to be taken from ground level. Many
changes are evident, with basically only the
two through lines left, although the station
seems to have survived with only minor
alterations. The ex-Great Northern line to
Louth lost its passenger services on
5 October 1970 and the section from Louth
to Grimsby, which was retained for freight,
closed completely from 3 October 1980.
Although the track was lifted, an active
preservation scheme is endeavouring to
restore services over the route. *Author*

Cleethorpes

Then: April 1958

This terminus station, which opened on 6 April 1863, was the most easterly point of the Great Central Railway. It was originally built as a single-track branch from Grimsby, but the growth in the amount of holiday traffic to the popular east coast resort gradually saw facilities extended. The station used to be extremely busy in the summer months with excursion traffic, and there were extensive carriage sidings. Class B1 No 61281 is pictured ready to leave with a local train.
Ian Allan Library (K3654)

Now: 9 November 1996

Mirroring the decline in the provision of railway facilities at other traditional resorts, much has disappeared at Cleethorpes. The carriage sidings have been lifted and the through services to London King's Cross, which were operated into the era of the 'Deltics' and the InterCity 125s until withdrawn in the 1980s, have succumbed. The station layout is still similar to that of the 1950s. Class 153 No 153328 is shown leaving on the 15.10 service to Barton-upon-Humber, whilst to the right a West Yorkshire PTE-liveried Class 158 No 158910 is being prepared for the 15.28 service to Manchester Airport. Locomotive-hauled trains are now quite rare at this destination. The station building on the right is now a pub/restaurant. *Author*

New Holland Pier

Then: July 1956
This fascinating station, situated at the end of a 500yd-long pier out into the Humber Estuary, opened on 1 March 1848. It was originally started by the Great Grimsby & Sheffield Joint Railway, which had become part of the Manchester, Sheffield & Lincolnshire Railway by opening. The Great Northern Railway had reached Grimsby by this time and so a through service from King's Cross to Hull, via the ferry from New Holland, became possible. During World War 1, the newest ships on the route (*Brocklesby*, *Killingholme* and *Cleethorpes*) were sent for war service, thereby extending the lives of the older ships (*Magna Carta* and *Grimsby*). Drive-on car facilities became available with the introduction of *Tattershall Castle* and *Wingfield Castle* in 1934 and *Lincoln Castle* in 1940. Here a locally-based 'B1' No 61328 is shown arriving with a nine-coach train of non-corridor stock, which suggests that there must have been plenty of passengers for the ferry. *Ian Allan Library (K3171)*

Now: 9 November 1996
Following the withdrawal of the three older ferries (two of which survive — *Tattershall Castle* on the Thames and *Lincoln Castle* at Grimsby), the last ferry to operate, as a result of the opening of the Humber road bridge was *Farringford* on 24 June 1981. This was an ex-Southern Railway diesel-electric vessel originally designed for the Lymington-Yarmouth service. The withdrawal of the ferry meant that New Holland Pier station no longer served a purpose and it was closed, resulting in a recast to the services to Barton-upon-Humber. Today the pier still exists, but it has been converted to a loading dock with a conveyor belt system. The track is still in existence under the conveyor, and the signalbox still stands. *Author*

New Holland Town

Then: 12 June 1981
This station was situated at the point where the pier extended out into the Humber. Services to the station commenced on 1 March 1848. There used to be a triangular junction at this point, linking the line to New Holland Pier with that from Barton-upon-Humber to Grimsby. A Class 114 unit prepares to leave for Cleethorpes just a couple of weeks before closure. *Author*

Now: 9 November 1996
With the closure of the Humber ferries, the train service was recast in June to operate direct from Grimsby to Barton-upon-Humber, and New Holland station was relocated by about 400yd. As can be seen, there have been dramatic changes, with the site of the station now occupied by a large feedstuffs factory. *Author*

Dunford Bridge

Then: August 1954
The station was opened on 14 July 1845 and was situated at the east end of the Woodhead Tunnel. The original tunnel was one of the greatest achievements of the early railway engineers, but was destined to be replaced by a new tunnel in connection with the electrification of the Manchester-Sheffield line. The new tunnel opened on 3 June 1954, and this photograph was taken two months later. It shows one of the then new Class EM1 (later Class 76) electrics about to haul dead steam locomotives — a 'B1' and a 'WD' — through the tunnel to Gorton Works for repair. *Kenneth Field*

Now: 13 August 1996
Passenger services along the Woodhead route ceased on 5 January 1970. Freight services over the route were withdrawn on 20 July 1981 amidst much controversy. Today the platform edge supports still exist as do the old concrete lamp standards, but little else, other than the trackbed, remains. The original single-bore tunnels were converted after 1954 to carry electricity cables through the Pennines; at 3 miles and 22yd in length the original tunnels were 44yd shorter than the new one. The new tunnel is still well maintained, pending possible further use by the electricity company. *Author*

Torside

Then: 18 April 1964
This section of the old Sheffield, Ashton-under-Lyne & Manchester Railway Woodhead route opened on 8 August 1844. One of the seven Class EM2 (later Class 77) Co-Co electric locomotives built for the Woodhead electrification scheme in 1954, No 27002, is shown passing *en route* to Sheffield. After withdrawal of the class in September 1968, all were sold for further operation with Netherlands Railways, where all (except ex-No 27005) remained in service until 1986. Three have been preserved. *Author*

Now: 13 September 1996
Following the withdrawal of passenger services over the route in January 1970, it was the intention to utilise the Woodhead route as the primary trans-Pennine freight artery. Much of the traffic was coal from the Yorkshire coalfield destined for the power stations of Lancashire. However, further rationalisation of the trans-Pennine routes led to the Woodhead route's complete closure in July 1981. Fifteen years on, the trackbed has been converted into a footpath up the valley. Unfortunately, the scene has not been enhanced by the erection of the electricity pylons. *Author*

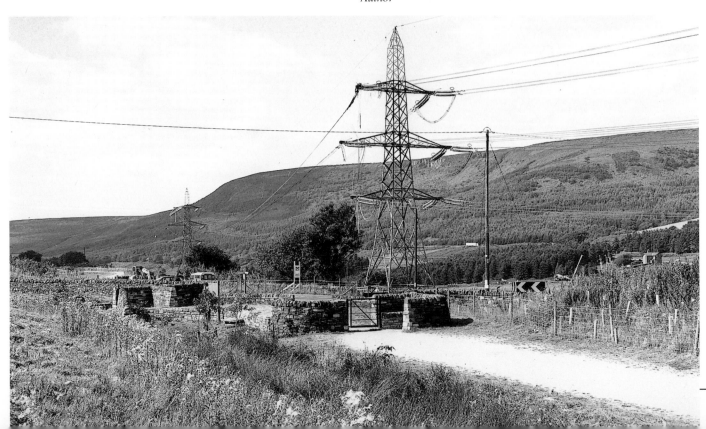

Hayfield

Then: 28 January 1967
The branch from New Mills to Hayfield was Great Central and Midland joint and opened on 1 March 1868. Freight services over the branch were withdrawn on 15 April 1963. With an air of dilapidation about the site indicating a none too prosperous future, a Metro-Cammell (later Class 101) DMU awaits departure. *Author*

Now: 13 September 1996
Passenger services were finally withdrawn on 5 January 1970 and the site has now become a car park, well laid out so that there is room to have picnics, etc. The building on the left is a shop as well as the Sett Valley Trail Ranger Post. *Author*

Guide Bridge

Then: Late 1950s
The first railway opened at Guide Bridge on 17 November 1841. It was the point where the Stockport-Stalybridge line bisected the route linking Manchester with Sheffield. The picture shows a Stanier 2-6-2T, No 40071, providing the motive power for a Stockport-Stalybridge local service. The train is standing in the eastern platforms underneath the 1,500V dc overhead of the Manchester-Sheffield-Wath scheme.
J. Davenport

Manchester London Road

Then: Mid-1950s
This station was opened on 8 May 1842 and was known for a few years as Store Street. It was eventually shared by the GCR and LNWR, and had 12 platforms plus one island platform, making a total of 14 in all. The GCR trains used mainly platforms Nos 1-4 for their local services and through expresses to Marylebone. These platforms were wired for 1,500V dc electrification as part of the Woodhead scheme in 1954. A couple of Robinson-designed Class C13 4-4-2s, No 67401 and 67431, which worked the suburban lines in the area, are shown at the end of the platforms. Both were built locally, one at Vulcan Foundry and the other at the GCR's Gorton Works, just a few miles down the line. They were withdrawn after the electrification of the local services in 1954. *K. Field*

Wrexham Central

Then: 27 September 1958
At one time Wrexham was served by the Great Central, Great Western and Cambrian Railways and the section of track north from the town to Hawarden represented the only stretch of railway owned in the Principality by a constituent of the LNER. The line had originally been built by the Wrexham, Mold & Connah's Quay Railway and had opened in 1866. It had fallen under the control of the MS&LR during Sir Edward Watkin's period of empire building and was connected to the remainder of the LNER network solely by the tracks of the Cheshire Lines Committee. This view, from the west, shows the lines of the Cambrian Railways stretching off, ironically, towards England and a connection with the main Cambrian route at Ellesmere.
T. Lewis

Now: 13 September 1996
The platforms on the east side of the station have now been taken out of use, with all services passing through the tracks on the right. Today the line is extremely busy at this point as it is used by all trans-Pennine services to and from Manchester Piccadilly, as well as the electric services to Hadfield and Glossop. The two routes split just to the north of the platform end. Many of the sidings have been lifted, except for those on the west side which are retained for engineering purposes. *Author*

Now: 3 October 1996
Now know as Manchester Piccadilly, this remains a very busy station, particularly since most of the trans-Pennine services were transferred from Victoria and Exchange stations. The life-expired dc electrification was replaced by more modern 25kV ac in 1984, although only the lines to Glossop and Hadfield remain of the ex-GC operation. West Yorkshire PTE Class 158 No 158908 is shown leaving on the 14.34 to Hull. *Author*

Now: 3 October 1996
The ex-Cambrian line to Ellesmere was to lose its passenger services on 10 September 1962 and to close completely beyond Pickhill at the same date. The section beyond Wrexham was to close progressively thereafter, with the final closure, to Abenbury, occurring in early May 1981. The station is now reduced to an unstaffed terminus surrounded by a car park. It still, however, enjoys an hourly service during the day to Bidston. These are usually worked by Class 142 Pacer units or, as here, by a Class 153. No 153363 is shown ready to leave for Bidston with the 16.33 service. There is currently a proposal to move the station a few hundred yards down the track, no doubt to make room for yet another shopping centre. *Author*

Penyffordd

Then: Early 1950s
This was one of the intermediate stations on the Wrexham, Mold & Connah's Quay Railway heading north from Wrexham. At this point a spur headed westwards to link in with the LNWR Mold-Chester line. The station nameboard proclaims 'Penyffordd for Leeswood'; the latter place is about one mile distant but is not directly rail served. A Stanier 2-6-2T No 40088 is captured arriving at the station with a train from the Bidston direction for Wrexham.
P. Ransome-Wallis

Now: 3 October 1996
In the pouring rain, Class 153 No 153316 arrives with the 16.32 from Bidston to Wrexham. Although semaphore signals are still in operation, a new signalbox has been built. The track layout has not really altered very much from that of 40 years ago, although the spur line no longer links in with the now closed route to Mold but provides access to the Castle Cement Works. The log trains to Shotton also use this route. *Author*

Liverpool Street

Then: 25 August 1948
This famous London terminus initially opened on 2 February 1874 for suburban services and was extended on 1 November 1875, when the former terminus at Bishopsgate closed. The design of the station was the work of Edward Wilson. In the post World War 2 years, Stratford shed used to keep the station pilot in immaculate condition. Class J69 0-6-0T No E8619 is seen in BR apple green livery waiting on the sidings between platform Nos 9 and 10 with a rake of assorted wagons. These locomotives were introduced in 1902. The locomotive was subsequently painted in BR lined black livery and then into Great Eastern blue with BR emblem and GER coat of arms. Withdrawn in 1961, it was to become part of the National Collection.
E. D. Bruton

Great Eastern Railway

The early history of the railways of East Anglia is one of frustrated ambition, where the major promoters often failed to achieve their aims. The Great Eastern itself was only formed on 7 August 1862, being the amalgamation of a number of earlier concerns. Of these the most important was the Eastern Counties Railway. The ECR dated from 1836 and was empowered to build a railway from London to Great Yarmouth. The first section, from Mile End to Romford, opened on 20 June 1839. The line reached Colchester in 1843. The line was built to the gauge of 5ft 0in, but was converted to standard gauge in late 1844. Despite the ECR's ambitions to build north of Colchester, it was another company, the Eastern Union, that constructed the line from there to Ipswich, which opened in 1846.

The Eastern Counties Railway, although unable to complete its route, was involved in a number of other projects, often without formal permission. On 1 January 1844 it leased the Northern & Eastern Railway. This company had also been authorised in 1836, this time to construct a line north towards Cambridge initially from Islington but later amended to a junction with the ECR at Shoreditch. The line opened in stages to Bishops Stortford between 1840 and 1842 and was again built to the 5ft 0in gauge. A branch to Hertford was opened in 1843, prior to the ECR taking a lease and the main line opened in stages to Brandon during 1845.

The ECR's mini (and unauthorised) empire expanded in 1848 with the absorption of the Norfolk Railway. This company had been established in 1845 by the merger of the Norwich & Brandon Railway and the Yarmouth & Norwich. The latter company had formed the first line into Norwich when it opened on 1 May 1844. The Norwich & Brandon line was opened in July 1845, with a connection to the Y&NR route being opened the following December.

The Eastern Union Railway line between Colchester and Ipswich opened in 1846. The EUR incorporated the Eastern Union & Hadleigh Junction Railway in 1847 and the Ipswich & Bury Railway in the same year. The Eastern Union reached Norwich in 1849, serving a second station, Victoria, in the city; a link was eventually constructed to the Norwich & Brandon line (1852) and Victoria station was to lose its passenger services in 1916. The EUR was to become part of the ECR network in 1854.

A later — 1859 — absorption by the ECR saw it take over the East Suffolk Railway. The ESR was based around the Halesworth, Beccles & Haddiscoe Railway (formed 1851; opened 1854 from Beccles to Haddiscoe) with the East Suffolk line, along with the branches to Framlingham and Leiston (later extended to Aldeburgh) opening on 1 June 1859.

Another important constituent of the GER was East Anglian Railways; this company had been formed in 1847 by the merger of three small companies: the Lynn & Dereham (formed 1845; opened 1846-48), the Lynn & Ely (formed 1845; opened 1846/47 with the Wisbech branch following in 1848) and the Ely & Huntingdon (formed 1845; opened 1847). This company was for a time operated by the GNR, but operation passed to the GER with its creation in 1862.

From these confused beginnings, the GER developed into an impressive network that, with the exception of the Midland & Great Northern in north Norfolk and the London, Tilbury & Southend in Essex, had a complete domination of East Anglia. It had close ties with the GNR, although a proposed merger to materialise, a relationship that was emphasised by the creation of the GN&GE Joint Committee for the route from Huntingdon to Doncaster. The railway could boast an impressive London terminus, Liverpool Street, first opened in 1874.

The GER continued to expand well into the 20th century through its involvement with, primarily, the Norfolk & Suffolk Joint lines, promoted with the M&GNJR. However, in 1923 the GER passed to the control of the LNER and gradually economic reality took hold. The interwar years witnessed a number of closures, such as the withdrawal of passenger services over the Ramsey East branch in 1930 and over the Mellis-Eye branch the following year. Lacking the heavy industry of Yorkshire and the northeast and with a relatively sparse population, it was inevitable that many of the GER lines would succumb in the decades after Nationalisation, when economic reality decreed that certain lines were unprofitable. The result has been that whole areas of the region are now bereft of railways as the lines to the north of the Norwich-Ely line were closed, as were the lines on the Suffolk-Essex border between Cambridge and Sudbury. The north Norfolk region is now served by a single branch, running from Norwich to Sheringham via Cromer. The main lines, from London to Norwich and London to Kings Lynn survive and are now electrified. Other routes to survive include the route from Ely/Cambridge to Ipswich and the lines to Great Yarmouth and Lowestoft from Norwich. Despite being long threatened. the East Suffolk line from Ipswich survives, although only after much rationalisation. The whole region is, however, criss-crossed with disused lines, many of which are gradually reverting to the agricultural land from which they emerged in the heady days of the railway mania.

Now: 27 January 1997
Wilson's station was threatened by the redevelopment of the adjacent Broad Street station, and only a campaign led by the former poet laureate, the late John Betjeman, saved the building. Although the area was redeveloped during the 1980s, the station itself was modernised and indeed extended in a style similar to that of the 1870s. Class 317/2 No 317366 is pictured here stabled in the station awaiting use in the evening peak. *Brian Morrison*

Seven Sisters Junction

Then: Undated

This station, located on the line from Hackney Downs north towards Enfield Town, is on the section of line — from Stoke Newington to Lower Edmonton — that opened on 22 July 1872. Seven Sisters was the junction for the GER branch to Palace Gates (opened from Seven Sisters to Green Lanes on 1 January 1878 and thence to Palace Gates on 7 October 1878) as well as a link to the Gospel Oak-South Tottenham line (opened 1 January 1880). Here an unidentified Class N7 0-6-2T enters the station with a train from Liverpool Street. *D. Lawrence*

Angel Road

Then: 29 April 1951

This station is on the main Liverpool Street-Cambridge line, which opened in 1840. The station, which was initially known as Edmonton and later as Water Lane, became a junction on 1 March 1849 with the opening of the line towards Enfield. This line lost it importance with the opening of the line through Seven Sisters, but retained some passenger services until 11 September 1939. A well-cleaned Class B17 No 61631 *Serlby Hall*, named after a country house near Retford, makes a fine sight as it heads the up 12.15 Ely-Liverpool Street express. No 61631 was withdrawn as a 'B17/6' in April 1959. The bracket signal in the background controlled the junction with the line towards Lower Edmonton. *J. F. Ayland*

Stratford Low Level

Then: 3 June 1961

The station is below the main Stratford station, which serves the GE main line between Liverpool Street and Colchester. The line to North Woolwich opened on 14 June 1847 and, in its prime, this route saw much traffic to and from London Docks. As the importance of the docks declined so too did the railway. Here Class N7/3 0-6-2T No 69725 has just arrived at the station with the 12.2pm service for North Woolwich. *J. C. Haydon*

Now: 11 February 1997
Class 315 No 315852 is shown working the 11.57 Liverpool Street-Enfield service. The signalbox is still in use, but I believe only when a train is required to take the link line to South Tottenham, which is hidden behind the third coach of the unit. The trackbed from where the picture was taken led to Palace Gates — closed to passengers on 7 January 1963 and to freight on 28 December 1964 — and some 20yd behind the photographer the bank ceases and all traces have been removed to make way for a housing estate. On the bottom left-hand side of the 'Then' picture can be seen the gradient post, the remains of which lie broken in the 'Now' shot. *Ken Brunt*

Now: 11 February 1997
The line to Edmonton closed completely on 7 December 1964. Class 322 No 322481, in Stansted Airport Express livery, is caught passing the station. *Ken Brunt*

Now: 27 January 1997
Since the massive redevelopment of the Docklands area, the railway is now enjoying a new lease of life, after major alterations which resulted in this section of the line being closed for about a year. The route now forms part of the very busy North London line, running right through to Richmond to the west of London.
Class 313s are the normal units used and No 313016 is shown arriving at the station with the 09.26 Richmond-North Woolwich service. A wall prevents an exact copy of the 'Then' photograph being taken, and the Jubilee Line extension has put the Low Level platforms in the middle of a building site. *Brian Morrison*

Temple Mills Yard

Then: 10 April 1954
This used to be the main marshalling yard for the Great Eastern lines in the London area, and is situated to the north of Stratford on the through Lea Bridge and Tottenham Hale line. Setting out from the yard 0-6-0 shunter No 12106 hauls a lengthy transfer freight consisting of box vans, open wagons, tanks and flat containers. *Brian Morrison*

Canning Town

Then: 15 June 1962
This is one of the intermediate stations on the Stratford Low Level-North Woolwich line, which opened on 14 June 1847. The now preserved 'N7' 0-6-2T No 69621 makes a fine sight as it leaves the station with the 7.10pm (SX) North Woolwich-Stratford Low Level service. *J. D. King*

Hertford East

Then: Undated
The Northern & Eastern Railway (later GER) reached Hertford with its branch from Broxbourne on 31 October 1843. This view, taken from a carriage window, shows 'N7/2' 0-6-2T No 69684 ready to leave with a train. The carriage sidings can be seen in the background. Until 1960, when electrified services started, there was a small shed, coded 30B, here. This had an allocation of around 13 'N7s' for working the trains to Liverpool Street. The shed was demolished in 1961. *G. H. Robin*

Now: 12 February 1997
The track layout has altered several times since 1954, and the current view shows the vast array of engineers' wagons that are stored here since the M11 link road forced the relocation of the engineers' sidings. The Foster Yeoman stone terminal is to the left and behind the photographer. The pylons have been relocated and additions made. The chimney, which was part of the wagons repair works, has gone and the site is now occupied by the new Spitalfields Market. The tracks out of sight to the extreme right of the picture are the through lines on which the Enfield Town-Stratford 'ghost' trains run. *Ken Brunt*

Now: 12 February 1997
Class 313 EMU No 313005, on the North Woolwich-Richmond service, passes the site of the old Canning Town station which was rebuilt in the 1930s. There have been four stations on this site and the present station is now on the other side of the road bridge in the distance and has interchange facilities with the Docklands Light Railway and the Jubilee Line extension. The tracks of the JLE are in the foreground; these were formerly the goods lines to the docks. The spot from which the 'Then' picture was taken no longer exists, as it was taken from the steps of the signalbox which straddled the goods lines on a gantry. *Ken Brunt*

Now: 8 February 1997
The station layout has hardly altered over the years, although the carriage sidings are now derelict. The signalbox still stands at the end of the platforms. Class 315 No 315817 is about to leave with the 13.17 service to Liverpool Street. Currently the service operates every half hour during the day. *Author*

North Weald

Then: 1953

This was one of two intermediate stations between Epping and Ongar and opened on 24 April 1865. Like the rest of the line, it passed to London Transport control after World War 2 and steam services were progressively replaced by electric operation. Evidence of the LT ownership is clear here through the roundels on the platforms, but there are, as yet, no signs of impending electrification. *Ian Allan Library (26997)*

Now: 29 September 1996

Steam operation of the Epping-Ongar shuttle ceased on 18 November 1957. For more than 30 years services continued, but increasing financial pressures brought the eventual closure of the section between Epping and Ongar in 1994. The track still survives and there are plans by a preservation society to reintroduce trains between Epping and Ongar. The station is privately owned but seems to have changed very little over 43 years except for the lifting of one track and the installation of electrification. The signalbox has been restored externally by the preservation society and the track still seems in reasonable condition, despite having been out of use for more than two years. *Author*

Ongar

Then: August 1956
The GER branch line to Ongar opened from Loughton on 24 April 1865. Although there were proposals prior to the outbreak of World War 2 for the service to be transferred to the control of the LPTB, it was only after the war that this took place. Between 1946 and 1948 the bulk of the ex-steam-operated lines were electrified as part of the Central Line, until only the Ongar shuttle was left to be steam-operated. Here Class F5 No 67212 has just arrived with a push/pull service from Epping. Although the service was run for London Transport, locomotives and rolling stock were BR. There was a small shed at Ongar.
Ian Allan Library

Now: 29 September 1996
Steam operation on the Epping-Ongar section ceased on 18 November 1957 when electrified services were inaugurated. The section was, however, well outside the London area and came increasingly under threat as budget pressures mounted. After a prolonged closure, services between Epping and Ongar ceased in September 1994. Following closure there are plans to reopen the line as part of a preservation scheme.
Author (both)

Maldon East & Heybridge

Then: April 1949
The branch from Witham, on the main line from Liverpool Street to Colchester, opened to freight on 15 August 1848 and to passengers on 2 October the same year. The station also became the terminus for the line from Woodham Ferrers, on the Southminster route, which opened on 1 October 1889. Ex-GER 'F5' 2-4-2T No 67189 (albeit still numbered LNER No 7189) prepares to leave the station with a train to Witham. Passenger traffic over the Woodham Ferrers route ceased on 10 September 1939. *Ian Allan Library (K165)*

Now: 29 September 1996
Passenger services on the Witham route were withdrawn on 7 September 1964 and freight followed on 18 April 1966. Behind the platform roof was an extremely impressive building. Unfortunately, it was not possible to stand in the same position as in the 'Then' photograph, so I had to take this rather restricted wide-angle view. Apparently the building had been in use as a restaurant in the recent past, but is currently vacant. It appeared that the site had been bought and was to be developed. *Author*

Wickford

Then: February 1955
The railways reached Wickford on 1 January 1889 with the opening of the Shenfield line; the line was extended to Southend on 1 October 1889. Here, a Class B12 4-6-0 No 61557, built by Beardmore & Co in 1921 and rebuilt as a 'B12/3 in 1934, is shown arriving with a train from Liverpool Street. *Ian Allan Library (K2458)*

Now: 30 September 1996
Apart from the electrification — completed on 31 December 1956 (initially at 1,500V dc and later at 25kV ac) — of the Southend line and the modernisation of the station booking hall, very little seems to have changed at the station. Class 321 No 321357 is shown leaving on the 09.39 to Liverpool Street, where, with one stop, it will arrive at 10.15 taking 36min for the 29-mile journey. *Author*

Southminster

Then: February 1955
The 16.5-mile branch from Wickford to Southminster saw freight services inaugurated on 1 June 1889 and passenger services exactly one month later. Class N7/5 0-6-2T No 69630, built at Stratford Works in November 1925 and, at the date of the photograph allocated to Stratford shed, it prepares to leave the terminus with a service for Wickford. *Ian Allan Library (K2459)*

Kelvedon Low Level

Then: 1950
The 10-mile-long light railway constructed by the Kelvedon, Tiptree & Tollesbury Pier Light Railway opened in two stages: from Kelvedon (on the Great Eastern main line where a separate station was provided) to Tollesbury on 1 October 1904 and then to the Pier on 15 May 1907. The line was worked by the GER. The main line was above the platform and behind the bushes, and the path to it can be seen to the left of the station building.
Ian Allan Library (24720)

Earls Colne

Then: 1953
The independent (until 1923) Colne Valley & Halstead Railway was opened in two stages: from Chappel via Earls Colne to Halstead on 16 April 1860 and thence to Haverhill on 10 May 1863.
Ian Allan Library (27310)

Now: 30 September 1996
The branch was electrified from 12 May 1986 and there is currently an hourly service. Some trains run through to Liverpool Street, whilst others require a change. Class 321 No 321336 *Freeman Allen* (named after the late railway author and son of Cecil J. Allen) prepares to leave with the 08.31 to Wickford. In addition to the passenger service, there is also a weekly nuclear flask train to Bradwell nuclear power station, the loading point being just outside Southminster station. As the line is singled, it means that a service train has to be cancelled when the flask train runs. *Author*

Now: 30 September 1996
Passenger services over the light railway were withdrawn on 7 May 1951 and the final freight traffic, over the Kelvedon-Tiptree section succumbed on 1 October 1962. No trace of the terminus remains today and the land it once occupied is at the side of a cultivated field. A Class 321 EMU can just be seen passing non-stop through the main line station. *Author*

Now: 30 September 1996
Passenger services between Chappel and Haverhill were withdrawn on 1 January 1962 and freight services were withdrawn progressively thereafter. The section between Chappel and Halstead closed completely on 19 April 1965. The station area and house have now been taken over by a company of glass manufacturers. *Author*

Marks Tey

Then: 30 July 1958

The Eastern Counties main line through Marks Tey to Colchester opened for freight traffic on 7 March 1843 and to passenger services on the 29th of the same month. The station became a junction with the opening of the branch to Sudbury on 2 July 1849. Here the branch train is being worked by a Class J15 0-6-0 No 65456. *F. Church*

Now: 30 September 1996

Both the main line and the branch remain operational, although the latter has again been cut back to serve Sudbury and the former has been electrified. The 15.30 Liverpool Street-Norwich InterCity express is seen in the down platform, having made an unscheduled stop due to signalling problems. DVT No 9709 heads the train with Class 86/2 No 86215 *Joseph Chamberlain* providing the power at the rear. A glance to compare the state of the track on the branch between the two pictures suggests a visit from the weedkiller train would be in order. *Author*

Bures

Then: 1953
This station was one of the intermediate stations constructed for the Marks Tey-Sudbury route which opened on 2 July 1849.
Ian Allan Library (27313)

Now: 30 September 1996
Despite being threatened, the Sudbury branch remains open and the station now sees an hourly service for most of the day. It is an unstaffed halt and, as can be seen, the station buildings have been demolished with the exception of the wooden structure closest to the camera. The 10.43 service from Sudbury, formed of Class 153 No 153311, is show arriving. The view is taken from the platform rather than from the trackside to show the scene more clearly. *Author*

Sudbury

Then: 6 July 1958
The branch from Marks Tey, on the main line to Colchester, opened on 2 July 1849 to a terminus. The station in Sudbury was relocated when the line was extended further northwards to Long Melford (on 9 August 1865) and thence to Cambridge and Bury St Edmunds. This is a view of the locomotive stabling point to the side of the station with two ex-GER Class J15 0-6-0s, Nos 65451 and 65477, in attendance. *Author*

Now: 30 September 1996
All services north of Sudbury ceased on 6 March 1967 and the station reverted again to being a branch terminus. The site of the locomotive stabling point is now overgrown and derelict. *Author*

Now: 30 September 1996
Although the old station is derelict, the new platform that was provided by Network SouthEast sees Class 153 No 153311 ready to leave on the 11.43 service to Marks Tey. *Author*

Long Melford

Then: April 1956
The railway north from Sudbury to Long Melford opened on 9 August 1865. At Long Melford the line diverged, with one route heading westwards to Haverhill and one heading north to Bury St Edmunds; these two routes opened on the same day. The junction can be seen at the extreme right of this photograph, which shows ex-GNR Class C12 4-4-2T No 67367 working a service from Bury St Edmunds.
Ian Allan Library (K2864)

Now: 30 September 1996
The line north to Bury St Edmunds closed to passengers on 10 April 1961 and to freight on 19 April 1965. The remaining route, through Haverhill to Cambridge, closed on 18 April 1966 to freight and to passengers on 6 March 1967. These closures meant that Sudbury once again reverted to being the terminus of a branch. Today the station buildings survive, having been converted into a private house. *Author*

Lavenham

Then: 1953
Both Long Melford and Lavenham can lay claim to superb medieval churches; in the railway age they were also connected by rail, since Lavenham was an intermediate station on the route between Long Melford and Bury St Edmunds. The line opened on 9 August 1865 and, as is evident, substantial station buildings were provided.
Ian Allan Library (27326)

Bury St Edmunds

Then: 2 August 1953
Bury St Edmunds was once an important railway centre. Railways first reached the town from the east in 1846 and these were extended westwards on 1 April 1854. Its importance was emphasised by the opening of the line to Long Melford on 9 August 1865 and that north to Thetford on 1 March 1876. The station has a particularly imposing exterior with twin towers at the west end. Here Gresley-designed 'K3' 2-6-0 No 61942 is shown at the head of a summer Saturdays Only Clacton-Birmingham train. Even by the date of this photograph rationalisation had started to set in with the closure to passengers (on 8 June 1953) of the line to Thetford. *F. Church*

Colchester

Then: 1950
Railway services reached Colchester with the opening of the Eastern Counties line towards London in March 1843. Under the aegis of the Eastern Union Railway, the line was extended to Ipswich on 1 June 1846 (freight) and 15 June 1846 (passengers). From the early openings, Colchester grew into a significant railway centre with a second station (St Botolphs) and the lines to Clacton and Walton heading east from the town. This view shows the station in the immediate postwar years; what looks like an ex-GER Class J69 0-6-0T can just be seen in the bay platform on the right-hand side.
Ian Allan Library (24718)

Now: 30 September 1996
Passenger services between Bury St Edmunds and Long Melford were withdrawn on 10 April 1961 and freight services followed on 19 April 1965. The changes here have been dramatic, with the station building and site incorporated into the premises of a company called Armorea Ltd. As can be seen, however, the arch of the road over bridge still survives. *Author*

Now: 30 September 1996
Although services remain along the main line from Cambridge towards Haughley Junction, the days of Bury St Edmunds as a junction have disappeared. The freight services over the line to Thetford ceased on 27 June 1960, whilst on 10 April 1961 passenger services to Long Melford were withdrawn. The line southwards was to close completely on 19 April 1965. The station itself has not altered much, save that the two through roads have gone and the passenger entrance has been refurbished. The locomotive shed (31E) closed in 1959. Class 153 No 153335 is caught leaving on the 14.00 Ipswich-Peterborough service. *Author*

Now: 30 September 1996
The up platform has been altered to allow through running expresses to overtake stopping trains, the station having been rebuilt and the lines through it electrified. The 16.30 Liverpool Street-Norwich train has just arrived at 17.17 in the pouring rain. Class 86/2 No 86220 *The Round Tabler* is providing the motive power at the rear. *Author*

Colchester St Botolphs

Then: April 1949
The second station in Colchester is situated at the apex of a triangle formed of lines running into the Colchester-Clacton route. The terminus station opened on 1 March 1866 and was initially an important destination for freight and parcels traffic. Its importance as a passenger destination grew with the development of the lines to Clacton and to Walton. *Ian Allan Library (K180)*

Now: 30 September 1996
Now renamed Colchester Town, the station remains open. It is served by trains on the Colchester-Clacton service, a reversal being necessary at this point. On a very wet and dark evening, Class 312 No 312720 arrives from Colchester's main station. *Author*

Thorpe-le-Soken

Then: April 1949
This is the junction of the line between Colchester and Clacton with the branch for Walton on the Naze. The original route reached Weeley on 8 January 1866. It was extended from there to Kirby Cross (the station after Thorpe-le-Soken) on 28 July 1866. It was finally extended to Walton on 17 May 1867. Thorpe-le-Soken became a junction on 4 July 1882 when the 4.5 mile line to Clacton was opened. Here a Class B2 'Sandringham' 4-6-0 No 61644 *Earlham Hall* is about to unite portions of the trains arriving from Clacton and Walton before heading towards Colchester. Wagons can be seen in the goods yard on the left. *Ian Allan Library (K175)*

Harwich Town

Then: 1949
The branch to Harwich from Manningtree was opened on 15 August 1854. Illustrated here is ex-GER Class N7/4 No 69612 ready to depart on an up train from the island platform. The extensive facilities here are a reminder that Harwich was once the railhead for the passenger ferries across the North Sea. *Ian Allan Library (K169)*

Now: 1 October 1996
The island platform has been removed and the sidings seemed to be little used. The last train ferries to the Continent have been withdrawn. The line was electrified in 1986 and, a decade on, Class 312 No 312703 is caught ready to leave on the 11.07 service to Ipswich. The train service during the day is roughly hourly. Today most of the freight and international passenger traffic uses the recently retitled Harwich International. *Author*

Now: 1 October 1996
Services over the route were electrified in 1959. The island platform is now the only one still in use and the goods yard has been converted into a car park. Class 321 No 321301 is ready to leave on the 09.55 from Walton on the Naze, which will form the stopping train to Colchester, whilst the unit on the right is the 10.00 from Clacton and forms a fast train to Liverpool Street, where it arrives at 11.24. *Author*

Ipswich

Then: 5 March 1960
The Eastern Union Railway provided Ipswich with its first railway link when it opened its line to Colchester on 1 June 1846 (freight) and 15 June 1846 (passengers). Heading northwards, the line towards Haughley Junction was formally opened on 7 December 1846. The two railways were linked in Ipswich by a 361 yd-long tunnel through Stoke Hill. Various disputes, however, meant that the site of the permanent station was not concluded until 1860. The town developed into an important railway centre. Class B1 4-6-0 No 61311 reverses through the station towards the shed, which was situated at the south end of the tunnel. On the right a Brush Type 2 passes with a Parkestone Quay-Whitemoor freight. *John C. Baker*

Felixstowe Town

Then: Undated (pre-1923)
The branch from Westerfield on the Ipswich-Lowestoft line to Felixstowe Town opened on 1 May 1877. It was initially operated by the Felixstowe Railway & Pier Co Ltd, but the GER took over operation two years later. This pre-Grouping scene sees a 4-4-0 (later LNER Class D15) ready to leave with an up train. *Ian Allan Library*

Now: 1 October 1996
Ipswich remains an important railway centre and in the station area the layout has not altered much, although electrification has made its presence felt. Today it is busy with both passenger and freight movements. Class 321 No 321445 is shown at the south end of the station ready to leave on the 12.30 service to Liverpool Street. It will cover the 68.75 miles in 74min with three stops. *Author*

Westerfield

Then: Early 1950s
Located a few miles east of Ipswich on the Lowestoft line, which opened on 1 June 1859, the station became a junction on 1 May 1877 with the opening of the branch to Felixstowe. Here Class B17/6 'Sandringham' No 61656 *Leeds United* passes the station with an up milk train. *R. C. Riley*

Now: 1 October 1996
Both the East Suffolk route to Lowestoft and the branch to Felixstowe remain open; indeed with the level of freightliner traffic coming off the latter it is unlikely that this location has ever been busier in railway terms. The station is still open and Class 153 No 153335 is caught as it leaves for Ipswich with the 13.10 service from Felixstowe. *Author*

Now: 1 October 1996
The town still has a passenger service from Ipswich and trains are normally formed of either Class 150/2 Sprinters or single-unit Class 153s. The original station site has now become a supermarket, although some of the station structures have been retained. The present station, which is a single platform, was immediately behind me when I took this photograph. *Author*

Wickham Market

Then: April 1949
This station is on the Ipswich-Lowestoft line, just south of the junction with the now closed branch to Framlingham. The line was opened on 1 June 1859. Class F3 2-4-2T No 7150 is shown against the warehouse, on a train which will form a service to Framlingham. The locomotive was withdrawn in October 1949 and never received its BR number.
Ian Allan Library (K1181)

Now: 1 October 1996
The station is still open and has staggered platforms; the platforms in use were behind me. The railway warehouse is now an antiques centre. Part of the original up platform has been abandoned as it is not required to accommodate the two-coach Sprinters that form the usual traction over the route. *Author*

Leiston

Then: 9 September 1955
The railways reached Leiston on 1 June 1859 with the opening of the branch line from Saxmundham on the East Suffolk line. Leiston was destined to remain the terminus of the branch for less than one year, as on 12 April 1860 it was extended to Aldeburgh. Class J15 0-6-0 No 65447 is seen working the branch passenger service. It is shown passing the Aveling Porter geared locomotive *Sirapite* which was owned by the famous local engineering company of Richard Garrett. *W. M. J. Jackson*

Now: 1 October 1996
After the closure of the line to passenger services on 12 September 1966 and the complete closure of the extension to Aldeburgh, the remains of the line to Leiston were and are retained as far as the Sizewell nuclear power station, which is located on the Aldeburgh side of the town. The nuclear flask trains run weekly, but my visit did not coincide with a working. As can be seen, the platform and station buildings still stand, and the latter are occupied. *Author*

Aldeburgh

Then: Undated
The branch from Saxmundham on the East Suffolk line to Leiston opened on 1 June 1859. It was extended to Aldeburgh on 12 April 1860. This photograph shows the station retaining its overall roof, which it lost before closure. *D. Raynford*

Now: 1 October 1996
Freight facilities at Aldeburgh were withdrawn from 30 November 1959 and the branch lost its passenger services on 12 September 1966. The line, however, remains open as far as Leiston to serve the Sizewell nuclear power station. I needed to visit the Station Hotel, which is to the left of the photograph, to seek advice as to where to stand to take a comparative picture. This was where I was instructed to stand, but there is little to remind you that the station once stood here, except that the road's name is Station Road. *Author*

Haughley Junction

Then: April 1949
The station nameboard indicates the importance that Haughley once claimed. It was (and is) the junction between the main line from Ipswich to Norwich with the line that heads westwards through Bury St Edmunds. It was also the junction for the independent Mid-Suffolk Light Railway. The picture shows a Class D16 'Claud' piloting a Class B17 'Sandringham' on a southbound train heading towards Ipswich. *Ian Allan Library (K188)*

Now: 30 September 1996
Both the Ipswich-Norwich route and the Bury St Edmunds line remain open, although the Mid-Suffolk Light Railway was to close on 28 July 1952 from Haughley to Laxfield. Haughley Junction station was closed on 2 January 1967, but the old station building can just be seen on the right of this picture. Sprinter No 150229 comes over the crossover off the Cambridge line and heads for Ipswich. *Author*

Hadleigh

Then: 1949
The seven-mile branch from Bentley to Hadleigh opened for freight on 21 August 1847 and to passengers on the following 2 September. Passenger services were withdrawn on 29 February 1932, a victim of competition from new bus services. Freight, however, continued to operated for a further 30 years. The somewhat dilapidated condition of the station tells its own story in this 1949 shot. *Ian Allan Library (18707)*

Now: 30 September 1996
Freight services over the branch were finally withdrawn on 19 April 1965. The station building still stands, but is boarded up. The land of the trackbed and the rest of the yard are now being developed with private housing. Note that the chimneypots have gone from the station's chimneys. *Author*

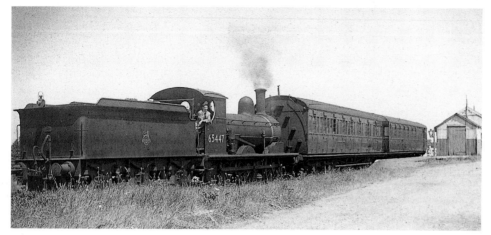

Laxfield

Then: 5 July 1952
The independent Mid-Suffolk Light Railway opened between Haughley and Laxfield on 20 September 1904. There were two other short sections opened, but these were shortlived. The light railway was 19 miles in length. On this date, towards the end of the railway's life, the passenger service was in the hands of Class J15 0-6-0 No 65447. *G. R. Mortimer*

Eye

Then: 1950
This was the terminus of a short branch from Mellis Junction on the main Ipswich-Norwich route. It was opened on 2 April 1867 and even by the date of this photograph passenger services had been withdrawn, these succumbing on 2 February 1931. *Ian Allan Library (24876)*

Now: 10 October 1996
The Mid-Suffolk Light Railway closed completely on 28 July 1952, some three weeks after the date of the 'Then' photograph. The line was subsequently lifted, although a short section has been relaid at Brockford to recreate a typical light railway of the early 20th century. I certainly needed the assistance of a local gentleman to find this site, which is just to the side of the road through the village. If one prods around in the undergrowth, it is still possible to find the platform edges. *Author*

Now: 1 October 1996
The Eye branch closed completely on 13 July 1964 and my thanks go to the directors of Grampian Country Foods for allowing me on to the premises to obtain the 'Now' photograph. It was decided by a small committee of employees that this is where I should stand to take the picture. I hope that it is correct, but what is certain is that the company now stands on the former railway land. *Author*

Mellis Junction

Then: June 1957
Situated on the main line between Ipswich and Norwich, railways first reached Mellis with the opening of the Finningham-Buston section of the route on 2 July 1849. The station became a junction with the opening of the Mellis branch on 2 April 1867. This photograph, from the mid-1950s, shows the old and the new side by side as a DMU (later Class 101) forms a Norwich-Ipswich service and a 'J17' 0-6-0, No 65542 (of Norwich shed), takes charge of the branch goods. *Dr Ian C. Allen*

Now: 1 October 1966
Mellis ceased to be a junction with the closure of the Eye branch on 13 July 1964. Mellis station itself closed on 7 November 1966. Evidence of both branch and main line platforms was to survive until the electrification of the route in the mid-1980s. The Great Eastern main line passes to the left of the fence and bushes, and the area of the old station once occupied by the branch to Eye has been partly redeveloped. *Author*

Norwich

Then: 6 August 1958

Railways arrived at Norwich in April 1844 with the opening of the Yarmouth & Norwich Railway. This was followed on 30 July 1845 by the opening of the Norwich & Brandon Railway which opened to a temporary terminus at Trowse; it was connected to the Norwich & Yarmouth line via a swing bridge over the River Wensum on 15 December the same year. The Eastern Union Railway built a line from Haughley Junction to a second terminus (Victoria); this line was

opened in stages in 1848 and 1849. A connection between Trowse Upper and Lower junctions was opened on 27 August 1851, allowing EUR trains into the original Thorpe station. The bridge to the south of the station used to be an excellent vantage point to watch the comings and goings at Norwich Thorpe. Here a Gresley Class J39 0-6-0 No 64731 departs with a freight train, whilst on the right a Brush Type 2 No 5513 stands at the fuelling point. The coaling stage of the steam shed can just be seen on the left. *F. Church*

Now: 2 October 1996

The land which the steam shed occupied on the left is now derelict and the diesel fuelling point has disappeared. The new locomotive maintenance depot is at Crown Point, just south of this bridge; it opened in 1983. Sprinter No 150227 makes its way out of the station under the wires on the 16.01 service to Lowestoft. *Author*

Norwich Thorpe (south)

Then: 21 July 1953

This fine study shows no less than three of the 'Britannia' class Pacifics that were allocated to Great Eastern services in the 1950s and which were always kept in excellent condition. In the background can be seen the steam shed's coaling tower and other locomotives are also visible. In 1950 there were 130 locomotives allocated here; this number had dropped to 93 in 1959, a total which included 21 'Britannias'. Closure of the shed came in 1962. *T. C. H. Hill*

Now: 2 October 1996

By this time there was little of interest to view from the platform end. The old steam shed area was empty and derelict. Electrification of the line to Norwich came with the official launch on 1 May 1987. *Author*

Norwich Thorpe

Then: 6 September 1954
The original station to serve Norwich was opened by the Yarmouth & Norwich on the site of the present Thorpe station on 30 April 1844. This station gained the suffix 'Thorpe' with the opening of the EUR's Victoria station later the same decade. The original station was soon to be insufficient for the services provided and the present Italianate building was opened to traffic on 3 May 1886. The 5.35pm train to Swaffham, formed of Class D16/3 No 62580 and six coaches, occupies most of platform No 5. At this date the locomotive was allocated to Yarmouth South Town. *R. E. Vincent*

Bungay

Then: 30 September 1956
This station was situated on the Beccles-Tivetshall Waveney Valley line. This 12.75 mile route was first promoted in 1851, but proved a struggle in being completed. The section from Tivetshall to Harleston opened on 1 December 1855. It was opened from Harleston to Bungay on 2 November 1860 and thence to Beccles on 2 March 1863. The line always struggled financially; indeed some stations were to close in the 1860s. The line lost its passenger services completely on 5 January 1953 and by the date of this photograph only freight services remained. In order to improve finances, a Light Railway Order for the line was issued on 15 November 1954. Here Class J15 0-6-0 No 65447 is ready to leave for Beccles with a rail tour. *H. C. Casserley*

Beccles

Then: April 1949
Situated on the East Suffolk line, Beccles was once an important railway junction. The first line to serve the town, running from Halesworth north to Haddiscoe (for a connection with the Yarmouth-Norwich route) opened to passengers on 4 December 1854. Beccles became a junction with the completion of the line to Lowestoft on 1 June 1859 and the construction was completed with the Waveney Valley line westwards to Bungay, which opened on 2 March 1863. This view, taken before any cuts occurred, shows Class F2 2-4-2T No 67112 providing the motive power for a Yarmouth motor-train, whilst on the right Class B12/3 No 61561 waits to depart with a Yarmouth-Liverpool Street service. *Ian Allan Library (K183)*

Now: 2 October 1996
The layout is basically the same in this part of the station, although today the station is much cleaner. Visible at the buffers in the background are Class 158 No 158850, Class 150 No 150237, Class 86/2 No 86240 (for the evening parcels train) and No 150213 can also just be seen. The background skyline is still largely unchanged, although trees have grown on the right. *Author*

Now: 2 October 1996
Despite the savings offered by the LRO, the line was not to survive. On 1 February 1960 the section between Harleston and Bungay closed completely. This was followed by the closure of the section from Ditchingham to Bungay on 3 August 1964. The remaining two sections — Beccles-Ditchingham and Tivetshall-Harleston — closed completely on 19 April 1965 and 18 April 1965 respectively. A new road to the left of the picture now occupies the trackbed and the bridge has vanished. *Author*

Now: 2 October 1996
The first casualty was the closure of the Bungay line to passenger services on 5 January 1953. This was followed by the closure to both passenger and freight services of the line to Haddiscoe on 2 November 1959. Beccles ceased to be a junction with the closure of the remains of the Bungay line on 19 April 1965. Today the five platforms that the station could once claim have been reduced to a single track and one platform serving the East Suffolk line from Ipswich to Lowestoft — but a shade of the station's former importance. Sprinter unit No 150255 calls with the 12.45 service from Ipswich to Lowestoft. As can be seen, the footbridge is still in use. *Author*

Beccles Swing Bridge

Then: 6 September 1952
Located to the north of Beccles on the line to Haddiscoe, this swing bridge over the River Waveney was on the section of line that opened on 4 December 1854. An ex-GNR Class C12 4-4-2T No 67357 is shown crossing the bridge with an up Yarmouth-Beccles stopping service.
R. E. Vincent

Lowestoft Central

Then: June 1954
Railways first reached Lowestoft with the opening of an 11.25 mile branch from Reedham. Freight services started on 3 May 1847 and passenger services on 1 July the same year. This was to be the only line into Lowestoft until the opening of the East Suffolk line from Beccles on 1 June 1859. A more direct link with Great Yarmouth came on 13 July 1903 with the opening of the Norfolk & Suffolk Joint line. A ex-GER Class F5 2-4-2T No 67218 is seen in the platform awaiting departure. The locomotive at this time was allocated to Yarmouth South Town shed (32D).
Ian Allan Library (K2274)

Yarmouth South Town

Then: June 1954
This station was served by both the Great Eastern Railway with services from Haddiscoe (which opened on 1 June 1859) and the Norfolk & Suffolk Joint (which opened on 13 July 1903). Here Class F5 2-4-2T No 67199 is pictured at the head of a local train. *Ian Allan Library (K2277)*

Now: 2 October 1996
The line from Beccles to Haddiscoe was to close completely on 2 November 1959 when both passenger and freight services over the route were withdrawn. This location took me 25min to walk to from where I had left the car after having driven down a farm track and when I eventually arrived, there was nothing to show for it. The bushes and undergrowth were so thick that I could not get to the river, which is just on the other side of the bushes. On my way back I discovered I could have driven to the spot! *Author*

Now: 2 October 1996
Apart from the closure of the direct line to Yarmouth (3 July 1967 to freight and 4 May 1970 to passenger services), Lowestoft retains its links to Beccles and Reedham. The station here today presents a sorry sight. The platform roofs have gone and the platform surfaces are in a poor state. Most of the sidings around the immediate station are still in place, but do not appear to be used. Sprinter No 150229 is ready to leave with the 12.56 departure. *Author*

Now: 2 October 1996
Services over the line to Haddiscoe were withdrawn on 2 November 1959, whilst freight services over the Norfolk & Suffolk Joint followed on 3 July 1967. Complete closure of the station came with the withdrawal of the passenger service to Lowestoft on 4 May 1970. The choice of viewpoint for the 'Now' photograph was the result of a conversation with a local gentleman, who assured me that I was in the correct position, although I have my doubts. This is, however, definitely the site of the station, Station Road being off to the right of the picture. As can be seen, very little remains to indicate that there was once a railway terminus here. *Author*

Yarmouth Vauxhall

Then: August 1960

Yarmouth could once claim three stations — South, Beach and Vauxhall. Of these only the latter is still open. Railways first reached Yarmouth with the opening of the Yarmouth & Norwich line on 30 April 1844. In August 1960 Class J19/2 No 64643 is shown bringing empty stock into the station for a summer Saturdays Only extra to the London Midland Region. *John C. Baker*

Now: 2 October 1996

Sprinter No 150213 is arriving with the 10.35 service from Norwich. The platforms are largely unaltered, but the area surrounding the station has changed dramatically. Gone are all the old lines used for storing carriages during the summer months, and the land thus released has been used for the building of a new road as well as an Asda supermarket. The signalbox still stands, but is now right up against a road bridge. *Author*

Haddiscoe

Then: 20 April 1996
This was once an important railway crossroads with two stations —
High Level on the line from Beccles to Yarmouth (which opened from
Beccles to Haddiscoe on 20 November 1854 and thence to Yarmouth on
1 June 1854) and Low Level on the Reedham-Lowestoft line (which
opened in 1847) — as well as links between the two routes. This is a
view of the Low Level station and shows the 12.26pm service from
Lowestoft Central to Norwich. *R. E. Vincent*

Now: 2 October 1996
Haddiscoe's importance as a railway junction declined with the closure
to passenger services of the Beccles-Yarmouth line on 2 November
1959 and the complete closure at the same time of the route north of
Haddiscoe. The section south from Haddiscoe to Aldeby closed in
February 1965. The original viewpoint was not possible as the
footbridge has been removed. The station is still served by the Norwich-
Lowestoft service, but is now reduced to a basic bus shelter. Note also
that the platforms that survive are now staggered. *Author*

Reedham

Then: 21 April 1954
Located on the Yarmouth & Norwich Railway's route, Reedham opened on 30 April 1844. Its importance grew with the opening of the branch to Lowestoft in 1847. Gresley Class K3 No 61926 is pictured calling at the station with a Norwich-Lowestoft train. After leaving Reedham, the train will turn right at the junction a few hundred yards further on and head over the swing bridge towards its destination. *R. E. Vincent*

Now: 2 October 1996
Comparison between these two photographs shows that very little has changed over the past 42 years. There were, however, no station staff on duty to meet the 09.03 service from Norwich to Lowestoft on this occasion. The train was formed of Sprinter No 150213. *Author*

Trimingham

Then: April 1953
This was one of a number of intermediate stations on the Norfolk & Suffolk Joint line between North Walsham and Cromer. The N&SJt was controlled by the GER and by the M&GNJR, although prior to the LNER's takeover of the M&GNR most trains over the route were operated by the latter. The section from North Walsham to Mundesley opened in 1898 and that from Mundesley, via Trimingham, to Cromer on 3 August 1906. Class D16/3 4-4-0 No 62617 was working the 1.10pm Sheringham-Norwich service towards the end of the line's life. It is seen departing from the station. *E. Tudenham/M&GN Circle*

Now: 15 November 1996
The Norfolk & Suffolk Joint line between Cromer and Mundesley closed completely apart from a short section at Cromer on 17 April 1953. The section from Mundesley to North Walsham survived until 1964. The top of the bridge is still in place, but the cutting on the south side has been filled in and the area is now used for the growing of sugar beet. *Author*

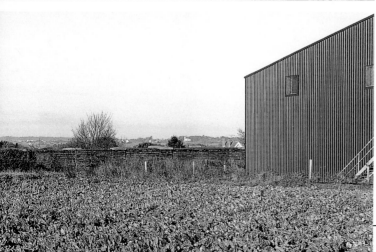

Fordham

Then: 26 May 1962
This station was located on the Newmarket-Ely route, which opened on 1 September 1879. The station became a junction with the opening of the lines to Cambridge on 2 June 1884 and to Mildenhall on 1 April 1885. Class 4MT No 43149 is pictured with a Midland & Great Northern Society special *en route* to Mildenhall. *D. Rees*

Now: 16 November 1996
Passenger services over the Cambridge-Fordham-Mildenhall route were withdrawn on 18 June 1962 and freight followed on 13 July 1964. The station at Fordham itself closed on 13 September 1965 and freight facilities were withdrawn the following year. There is very little one can say about the current site; everything has vanished of the old station and goods yard and all that is left is an automatic barrier across the road. *Author*

Brandon

Then: 1953
The line from Ely to Norwich Trowse through Brandon opened on 30 July 1845. Brandon was one of three intermediate stations between Ely and Thetford and was provided with staggered platforms.
Ian Allan Library (27305)

Now: 15 November 1996
Although freight facilities were withdrawn from the station on 18 April 1966, Brandon remains open to serve trains on the cross-country route from Ely to Norwich. The staggered platforms remain, as do the station buildings on the Norwich platform. The buildings on the Ely platform have been replaced by a bus shelter. The goods shed has gone. Class 158 No 158797 is shown arriving with the 13.43 from Norwich to Liverpool; it will reach its ultimate destination at 19.30. *Author*

Thetford

Then: 31 March 1962
Thetford was and is one of the most important towns of the region. The railway opened on 30 July 1845 and on 1 March 1876 the town became a junction with the opening of the line south to Bury St Edmunds. However, by the date of this photograph the Bury line had already closed (on 8 June 1953 to passengers and on 27 June 1960 to freight). 'Britannia' class Pacific No 70003 *John Bunyan*, then allocated to March shed, calls at the station with the 'Great Eastern Commemorative Steam Tour' organised by the RCTS. It is shown at the west end of the station ready to leave for Ely. At the end of the year No 70003 joined many of the other 'Britannias' at Carlisle Kingmoor.
Ian Allan Library (4930)

Mildenhall

Then: 30 November 1957
The branch from Cambridge to Mildenhall opened to Fordham on 2 June 1884 and thence to Mildenhall on 1 April 1885. Class J15 0-6-0 No 65438 is waiting to leave with a train for Cambridge. The branch became well known towards the end of the 1950s as one of the last haunts of the ex-GER 2-4-0s, of which No 62785 (now preserved as part of the National Collection) was the last, being withdrawn in December 1959. *L. King*

Now: 15 November 1996
Passenger services over the Mildenhall branch ceased on 18 June 1962 and freight was withdrawn on 13 July 1964. The fine station house, which seems very large for the relative unimportance of the branch, has now passed into private ownership. It has been beautifully restored and the grounds landscaped. *Author*

Now: 15 November 1996
The station enjoys an hourly service during the day from Norwich through to Liverpool using Class 158 units. No 158844 is shown arriving at 12.54 on the 08.52 departure from Liverpool. The fine signalbox is still in use. *Author*

Dereham

Then: 2 February 1973
This used to be a busy railway centre, with lines running north to Fakenham, south to Wymondham and west to Swaffham. The first line to reach the town opened from Wymondham on 7 December 1846 to freight and to passengers on 15 February 1847. The route from Swaffham opened in two stages: Swaffham-Sporle on 26 October 1847 and Sporle-Dereham on 11 September 1848. Finally, the line was extended from Dereham to Fakenham on 20 March 1849. In the days of Norwich-King's Lynn trains, these used to reverse in the station, whilst goods traffic was able to use the third side of the triangular junction to avoid the station. By the date of this photograph passenger services had already been withdrawn (from Dereham to Wells on 5 October 1964, to King's Lynn on 9 September 1968 and to Wymondham on 6 October 1969) whilst freight had also been withdrawn from the Swaffham line (on 30 June 1966). On a dismal day in early 1973 Brush Type 2 No 5587 (later Nos 31169/31457) does some shunting with the freight from Fakenham to Norwich.
C. Price

Takeley

Then: 1952
This station was located to the east of Bishop's Stortford on the line that provided a link, via Braintree, to the main line from Liverpool Street to Colchester at Witham. The line opened on 22 February 1869. Here one of the ex-GER Class F5 2-4-2Ts No 67211 calls at the station with a train for Witham (as indicated on the bunker). The 'F4s' and 'F5s', built between 1885 and 1909 at Stratford, could be seen all over the GER system, although some eventually finished up working the St Combs branch in northeast Scotland; in fact, the last of the class, No 67157, finished its days as the Inverness Works pilot. *D. Trevor Rowe*

Braintree

Then: 13 August 1956
The line between Bishop's Stortford and Witham opened on 22 February 1869. Class F6 2-4-2T No 67228, built at Stratford in June 1911, has arrived with the 3.53pm from Witham. Passenger services over the route west of Braintree had been withdrawn (except for excursions) on 3 March 1952, although freight continued to serve the route. The Braintree-Witham section went over to DMU and railbus operation. Despite being listed for closure in the Beeching Report, it survived.
D. Holmes

Now: 15 November 1996
The freight service over the Wymondham-Dereham-Fakenham line was gradually curtailed until complete closure. The station still stands and the railway area has not been developed. The buildings are the headquarters of the Mid-Norfolk Preservation Society, which aims to reopen the line to Wymondham, the track being in existence for much of the way. Most of the stock is currently stabled at Yaxham, and includes two Class 20s, five Mk1 coaches and a Class 121 diesel unit. Other items are at Dereham. Dereham station will make a fine site for a preservation line headquarters, with plenty of space for storage sidings. *Author*

Now: 29 September 1996
Passenger services over the route ceased on 3 March 1952 with the exception of the Braintree-Witham section that was eventually electrified. Freight over the section to Dunmow, including Takeley (which had lost its freight facilities on 18 April 1966), ceased on 1 April 1969. The trackbed is now a walkway and the station house seemed to be in a reasonable state of repair, although not permanently occupied. With the continuing development of the area, I am sure that the line could have provided a well-used link between the two ex-GER main lines had it survived. *Author*

Now: 29 September 1996
Following the line's escape from closure, traffic grew and it was electrified in 1977. It now enjoys an hourly service during the day to Liverpool Street, with extra trains during the rush hour. The 41.75 mile journey is covered in 64min. Here Class 321 No 321324 is shown leaving on the 17.17 train. Freight operation over the section westwards to Felstead ceased on 1 April 1969. *Author*

Linton

Then: April 1961
This station was situated about 12 miles east of Cambridge on the line towards Bartlow and Long Melford. The line opened from Cambridge to Haverhill on 1 June 1865. Ex-GER Class J15 0-6-0 No 65478 is seen leaving the station on a Cambridge University Railway Club engine driving special. *G. D. King*

Bartlow

Then: 16 April 1949
Located to the southeast of Cambridge on the line towards Long Melford, Bartlow was also the junction for the line through Saffron Walden to Audley End. The line opened from Cambridge to Haverhill via Bartlow on 1 June 1865. It became a junction with the opening of the Audley End line on 22 October 1866. Ex-GER 'J17' No 65575, but retaining 'LNER' on the tender side, is shown passing through the station with a goods train to Sudbury. *W. A. Camwell*

Haverhill North

Then: Undated
The town of Haverhill was originally provided with two stations: one for the Great Eastern line between Cambridge and Sudbury and one as the terminus of the Colne Valley & Halstead Railway. This was the ex-GER station. The line from Cambridge to Sudbury opened in two stages: from Cambridge to Haverhill on 1 June 1865 and thence to Sudbury on 9 August 1865. *Ian Allan Library (24820)*

Now: 15 November 1996
Passenger services over the Cambridge-Long Melford line ceased on 6 March 1967, freight over the route having been withdrawn on 31 October 1966. The station house has now been surrounded by a factory which can just be seen in the background of the picture, but nothing else remains at this location. *Author*

Now: 29 September 1996
Passenger services between Bartlow and Audley End ceased on 7 September 1964 and those over the Cambridge-Long Melford route on 6 March 1967. Freight operations over the Audley End route had ceased on 28 December 1964 and those between Cambridge and Long Melford followed on 31 October 1966. The trackbed now appears to be used by local farmers, nature having taken over. The station is now a private house, located behind the photographer. *Author*

Now: 29 September 1996
The line closed to freight services on 31 October 1966 and to passengers on 6 March 1967. The site is derelict, although signs can still be seen in the undergrowth of the platforms. A wide road leading to the old yard area, which is now a dead end, is still called Station Road. The old warehouse buildings were being used by local industries. *Author*

Audley End

Then: 30 May 1953
A delightful branch line picture shows ex-NER 0-4-4T No 67269, unofficially known as *Lucy Belle*, at the branch platform at Audley End with a service to Saffron Walden. The line from Audley End to Bartlow opened as far as Saffron Walden on 21 November 1865 and thence to Bartlow on 26 October 1866. Audley End provided a connection into the main Cambridge-London route. *R. E. Vincent*

Now: 29 September 1996
The line eventually went over to railbus operation, but even this was not enough to spare it and all passenger services were withdrawn on 7 September 1964. Freight traffic over the route ceased on 28 December 1964. The area once occupied by the branch has now been made into a large car park for commuters into London. It was empty on the day of my visit, it being a Sunday. *Author*

Cambridge North

Then: 19 September 1959
A superb picture full of interest shows Class B17/6 4-6-0 No 61659 *East Anglian* heaving with a train for Ely, while a Brush Type 2 (later Class 31) arrives with a freight from the north. Behind the signalbox can be seen locomotives parked in the shed yard and the coaling stage. This 'B17' along with No 61670 *City of London* was streamlined in 1937 to a design similar to that of the 'A4' Pacifics. The streamlining was eventually removed in 1951. *J. A. Coiley*

Now: 29 September 1996
The fine location from Mill Road bridge to the north of the station has now been ruined by the electrification of the line to King's Lynn. Class 158 No 158847 leaves the station under the wires on the 13.15 (SuO) service to Liverpool Lime Street, where it was due to arrive at 18.26. *Author*

Cambridge North (looking north)

Then: 12 May 1953
A dirty March-based 'Austerity' 2-8-0 No 90075 approaches Cambridge with a train from the north. The signalbox at Coldham can just be seen in the background. *Author*

Now: 29 September 1996
Electrification and some track rationalisation have altered this location. In the background to the right can be seen some Class 317 EMUs and a Class 158 parked up. To the left the gasometer is still visible. *Author*

Ely South

Then: 16 July 1960
The railways arrived at this busy centre on 30 July 1845 with the opening of the line from Newport (south of Cambridge) to Brandon. This route was followed with lines to March (opened to freight on 10 December 1846 and to passengers on the following 14 January), to King's Lynn (26 October 1847), to Sutton (16 April 1866) and to Newmarket (1 September 1879). Surrounded by a fine variety of signal gantries, of which there were many around the station area until electrification, 'Britannia' Pacific No 70035 *Rudyard Kipling* is shown ready to restart a Norwich-Liverpool Street express. *S. Creer*

Now: 16 November 1996
Although the line to St Ives has closed (losing its passenger services on 2 February 1931 and freight on the section between Ely and Sutton on 13 July 1964), Ely is still a very busy centre. Trains are mainly formed of Class 158 DMUs or Class 317 EMUs, but there is also still some freight traffic. The 11.39 departure to King's Cross is pictured formed of Class 317 No 317355. These services are soon to be taken over by the new Class 365s. *Author*

Earith Bridge

Then: 1 August 1955
This station was situated on the Ely-St Ives line. The line opened from Ely to Sutton on 16 April 1866 and thence to St Ives on 10 May 1878. Passenger services were withdrawn over the route on 2 February 1931, but excursions continued to operate. During the 1950s two trips annually were operated, one to Yarmouth and one to Hunstanton. This photograph of ex-GER Class J15 No 65457 arriving at Earith Bridge shows one of these excursions and explains the large number of passengers on the platform some 24 years after the loss of normal passenger services. I wonder if the locomotive ran through to its destination?
T. P. Paisley

Chippenham Junction, Newmarket

Then: 27 October 1951
The line from Newmarket to Bury St Edmunds opened on 1 April 1854 and a junction was created here with the opening of the line to Ely on 1 September 1879. There was also the third part of the triangular junction, allowing access from Newmarket towards Fordham, but this closed on 13 September 1965. Here a Class B17 'Sandringham' No 61653 *Huddersfield Town* is shown coming off the Ely line with a train for Colchester.
A. D. Edwards

March

Then: May 1961
Railways came to March with the opening of the lines to Ely and Peterborough (both opening to freight on 10 December 1847 and to passengers on 14 January 1848). The town became a junction with the opening of the lines to Wisbech (3 May 1847), to St Ives (on 1 February 1848) and to Spalding (on 1 April 1867). The last-named route was ultimately to form part of the GN&GE Joint route. Just to north of the station, on the Spalding line, was Whitemoor Yard, which was the main yard for sorting traffic over a wide area and the location of an important steam shed. In 1950 the shed had an allocation of 161 locomotives, which by 1959 had only reduced to 131. The steam shed closed in 1963 and was succeeded by a depot for the replacement diesels. Local 'K1' class 2-6-0 No 62040 pauses with one van prior to departing eastwards. The platforms for the joint GN&GE line can be seen on the right hand side; these tracks also gave access to Whitemoor Yard. *J. C. Baker*

Now: 16 November 1996
The section through Earith Bridge was the first part of the route to be closed completely (on 6 October 1958). Thereafter freight services continued to operate on both stubs from Ely and from St Ives, but these were withdrawn on 13 July 1964 and 5 October 1964. This location caused me some difficulty in finding; in fact I have had to rely on some locals to tell me where to stand. I hope they were right as there is nothing to identify the location specifically. Behind me is a bridge over the river and a cottage with a plaque recording the 1876 Sutton Bridge Railway Co, so I assume that the line must have been here. *Author*

Now: 16 November 1996
Getting to this location caused some difficulty as I had first to get permission from a local landowner, who was out shooting with friends near the spot, and then get permission from the racehorse training company which owns the road that led ultimately to the location. When I got there, I was completely baffled as to how the 'Then' picture was taken, as there was no height to get the viewpoint other than from the branches of a large oak tree, and even that was not in the correct position! So I have taken the picture from the road overbridge. Class 153 No 153311 is working the 09.43 Ipswich-Peterborough service. *Author*

Now: 18 January 1997
Today the station, which is very well kept, enjoys a frequent service of Sprinters between Norwich and Cambridge and the Midlands and north. There has been some rationalisation; the line to St Ives has closed completely (on 6 March 1967), passenger services over the Wisbech line succumbed on 9 September 1968, although freight services still operate, and the GN&GE Joint line closed north of Whitemoor Yard on 28 November 1982. Class 150 No 150229 calls at the station with the 12.14 Peterborough-Ipswich train. The Joint platforms still exist, although are not used, and a single line heads for what little is left of Whitemoor Yard and the Wisbech branch. *Author*

Peterborough East

Then: 24 June 1954
The GER line reached Peterborough with the opening of the line from Ely and March on 10 December 1846 (freight) and 14 January 1847 (passengers). Although the station was quite small, there was an extensive yard. Despite being built by the Eastern Counties Railway — predecessor of the GER — Peterborough East was first used by trains of the London & Birmingham Railway (LNWR) on its line in from Northampton, which opened on 2 June 1845. Also operating into East station were the Midland trains from the Stamford line, which opened on 2 October 1846. Here an ex-LMS Compound 4-4-0 No 41097 is shown arriving with a train. Note the impressive signalbox above the platforms. *R. E. Vincent*

Now: 18 January 1997
The station closed on 6 June 1966 with the withdrawal of passenger services over the former LNWR route. Freight facilities had been withdrawn slightly earlier, but the station was retained for parcels traffic until December 1970. The site has changed out of all recognition, although the line still sees plenty of traffic. Class 158 No 158852 is caught forming the 13.05 Cambridge-Birmingham New Street service. *Author*

Stoke Ferry

Then: 12 July 1959
The seven-mile branch from Denver, on the Ely-King's Lynn line, to Stoke Ferry opened on 1 August 1882. It lost its passenger services as long ago as 22 September 1930. A rare subsequent visit of a passenger train occurred on this occasion when an LCGB special visited the branch behind ex-GER Class J69/1 0-6-0T No 68566. This tour included a veritable feast of Great Eastern motive power, including a 'B12' 4-6-0, a 'D16' 4-4-0, an 'E4' 2-4-0 and a 'J15' 0-6-0 as well as the 'J69'. *Author*

Wisbech

Then: 27 July 1952
The town of Wisbech was served by both the GER and the M&GNJR. This was the ex-GER station which was situated on the King's Lynn-March line. The first link to the town came with the opening of the line to March on 3 May 1847; the line to King's Lynn followed on 1 February 1848. Class D16/3 4-4-0 No 62618 is seen at the station with a train for March consisting of a considerable variety of rolling stock. *P. H. Wells*

Now: 16 November 1996
This location proved extremely difficult to find, and I had to seek assistance from the locals. Passenger services over the March-King's Lynn line were withdrawn on 9 September 1968, at which time the line between Wisbech Goods Junction and Magdalen Road, on the Ely-King's Lynn line, closed completely. The whole station area has been redeveloped and the site is now occupied by an old people's home. There is still a railway presence to the town, however: a freight-only link survives from the outskirts to March. *Author*

Now: 15 November 1996
Freight services over the branch beyond Abbey & West Dereham to Stoke Ferry were withdrawn on 19 April 1965. More recently the remainder of the branch has closed. When I visited the site for this photograph, the station house was well maintained as the office for this local timber company, which had also taken over the yard area. *Author*

Upwell

Then: 1937
The Wisbech & Upwell Tramway was unusual in Britain in being a roadside line. It opened from Wisbech to Outwell on 20 August 1883 and thence to Upwell on 8 September 1884. Between 1883 and 1897 six tram locomotives — designated by the LNER as Class Y6 — were built to the design of T. W. Worsdell; two of these lasted until 1952 when they were replaced by Drewry diesel shunters which, like the tram engines, were fitted with casing to protect the coupling rods. The three diesels, built in May 1952, were originally numbered 11100-11102 and subsequently became Nos D2200-2202. Although a passenger service was operated over the line, this had ceased on 2 January 1928, almost a decade before this view of the overgrown track at Upwell.
Ian Allan Library (L&GRP 6606)

King's Lynn

Then: 1950
Railways reached King's Lynn with the opening of the first section of the Lynn & Ely Railway on 29 October 1846 (the line was completed through to Ely in 1847) and the town's importance as a railway centre grew thereafter with the opening of lines towards Narborough (29 October 1846), Hunstanton (3 October 1862), Sutton Bridge (1 November 1864) and Fakenham (16 August 1879). This illustration shows the scale of the station at King's Lynn immediately after Nationalisation. There was also a steam shed here, which in the 1950s had about 47 locomotives allocated. With its docks, King's Lynn always generated a great deal of freight traffic.
Ian Allan Library (23534)

Swaffham

Then: March 1962
Swaffham was the junction on the King's Lynn-Dereham line where the line south towards Thetford deviated. The King's Lynn-Swaffham-Dereham line opened in stages: King's Lynn-Narborough on 27 October 1846; Narborough-Swaffham on 10 August 1847; Swaffham-Sporle on 26 October 1847; and Sporle-Dereham on 11 September 1848. Swaffham became a junction in 1875 with the opening of the line to Watton. This exterior shot was taken when all the services still survived.
Ian Allan Library (K4924

Now: 16 November 1996
Freight services over the tramway ceased
on 23 May 1966. The station yard at
Upwell has now been developed with
houses and the town's health centre.
However, behind the point from where I
took this photograph it is still possible to
determine the route of the old trackbed.
Author

Now: 2 October 1996
Today the only passenger services to
King's Lynn are the electrified services
over the line south to Ely and Cambridge.
Electrification of the services came in 1982.
The station is now well kept and the car
park has been extended over some of the
old platform areas. On this occasion the
18.05 service to King's Cross was ready to
depart, formed of Class 317 No 317311.
Author

Now: 2 October 1996
Passenger services between Swaffham and
Thetford were withdrawn on 15 June 1964
and at the same time the section south of
Watton was closed completely. The section
from Swaffham to Watton lost its freight
services on 19 April 1965. Freight was
withdrawn from the Middleton Towers-
Dereham route on 30 June 1966 and the
line through Swaffham was to close
completely with the withdrawal of
passenger services from King's Lynn to
Dereham on 9 September 1968. As can be
seen, the building is still in excellent
condition and is occupied today by the
Merle Body Centre. The old goods
warehouse also still exists and is occupied.
Author

Wolferton

Then: 1953
This was one of five intermediate stations on the King's Lynn-Hunstanton line, which opened on 3 October 1862. The station is situated on the Royal Estate at Sandringham and was used regularly by members of the Royal Family when visiting the estate. As is evident in this photograph, the station was inevitably kept in excellent condition.
Ian Allan Library (27318)

Now: 14 November 1996
The Hunstanton line closed to freight services on 28 December 1964 and to passengers on 5 May 1969. Since closure, King's Lynn has become the railhead for members of the Royal Family travelling to Sandringham. Almost 30 years after closure, the buildings remain in reasonable condition. The house on the up (ie left) side is now privately owned, whilst the buildings on the down side are part of a railway museum which specialises in 'Royal' train travel. *Author*

Hunstanton

Then: 1931
The 15-mile line from King's Lynn to Hunstanton opened on 3 October 1862. At its peak the station could lay claim to through services to London, and to a considerable amount of holiday traffic. The picture was taken from a road bridge that has subsequently been demolished and clearly shows the layout of the station with its two island platforms. *Ian Allan Library (8965)*

Now: 14 November 1996
Despite the importance of the town as a summer resort, the line lost its freight services on 28 December 1964 and its passenger services on 5 May 1969. Following closure the station site has been cleared and converted into a car park. The size of the car park indicates that the resort must still be visited by large numbers of tourists in summer months, but on this occasion it contained only three cars and the town was extremely quiet. *Author*

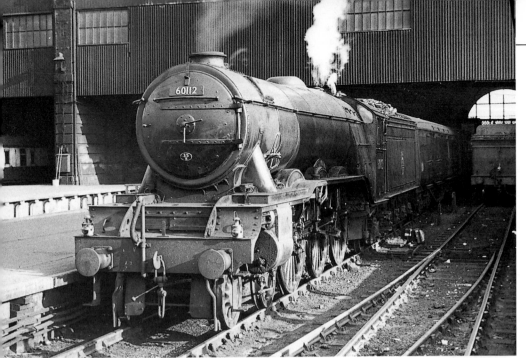

King's Cross

Then: 5 July 1952
The 9.15pm relief for the 9pm 'Aberdonian' awaits departure from platform No 7 at King's Cross behind Class A3 Pacific No 60112 *St Simon*, which was allocated to Grantham at the time. *St Simon* was named after the racehorse, owned by the Duke of Portland, which won the Ascot Gold Cup in 1884. The locomotive received a double chimney in 1958 and the German-type smoke deflectors in October 1962. The train included through coaches for Fort William and once carried the title of the 'Highwayman'. *Brian Morrison*

Now: 22 February 1997
Departing from King's Cross in a cloud of exhaust probably greater than would have emanated from the 'A3' Pacific, InterCity 125 power car No 43118 (once named *Charles Wesley*) heads the 14.00 service to Aberdeen. The power car is in the new GNER livery, but the stock still carries the standard InterCity colours. Many changes are apparent, not least of which is the removal of the lower section of the roof drop. *Brian Morrison*

Holloway Bank

Then: 11 July 1953
Class B17/6 No 61652 *Darlington* is shown drifting down the bank towards King's Cross with an up 'Cambridge Buffet' express. The locomotive was rebuilt as a 'B16/7' in March 1948 and survived until September 1959. *Brian Morrison*

Great Northern Railway

With some 1,051 miles at the Grouping in 1923 (excluding its share in the Great Northern & Great Eastern, the Cheshire Lines Committee and other jointly controlled lines), was the third largest of the LNER's English constituents. The GNR was incorporated in 1846 with the intention of building a main line from London to York and a line from Peterborough through Lincolnshire to Bawtry.

The first section of line, from Peterborough to Lincoln, opened on 17 October 1848. This was followed on 4 September 1849 by the line between Retford and Doncaster and on 7 August 1850 by the line from London — initially Maiden Lane but King's Cross opened on 14 October 1852 — to Peterborough. The final link of the line between London and Doncaster came with the opening of the link between Retford and Peterborough in 1852 (15 July for freight and 14 October for passenger services). Through the involvement of George Hudson, the GNR avoided the need to build an independent line to York.

Linked with the GNR at Boston was the East Lincolnshire Railway, which was incorporated in 1846 for the construction of a line from Grimsby to Boston. It was opened from Louth to Grimsby on 1 March 1848, from Louth to Firsby on 4 September 1848 and thence to Boston on 1 October the same year. Although the line was operated by the GNR, the East Lincolnshire Railway retained its nominal independence until the Grouping of 1923. The GNR and its allies continued to expand in Lincolnshire. These included the short branch from Firsby to Spilsby, which opened in 1868, the line from Firsby through Wainfleet to Skegness (which opened in two stages in 1871 and 1873), the Horncastle branch (1855), Louth-Bardney (1876) and Louth-Mablethorpe (1877). Also in Lincolnshire, Essendine became a significant junction with the branch to Stamford and the line northwards to Sleaford.

Further south, the GNR line from Hitchin to Shepreth was opened in two stages in 1850 and 1851; through a connection with the Eastern Counties Railway, access was gained to Cambridge. From Stevenage, the Hertford loop (opened to passenger services between Cuffley and Stevenage in 1924 although constructed under an act of 1898) an alternative route to King's Cross. From Hatfield three routes radiated — to St Albans, Dunstable and towards Hertford — whilst suburban lines were built to High Barnet, Alexandra Palace and Edgware.

In the Midlands, the GNR gained access to the Nottinghamshire coalfield through the line from Grantham to Nottingham (opened 15 July 1850). From Bottesford a GNR line headed north to form a connection at Newark and a joint GNR/LNWR route headed south (opened in stages during 1879). Through this line the GNR gained access to its own line into Leicester Belgrave Road (opened 1 January 1883). From Nottingham the GNR metals stretched north to Shirebrook, running parallel with both the Midland and Great Central metals, and west through Kimberley to Derby and Egginton Junction (1878), where a connection was made with the North Staffordshire Railway. An isolated section, access being gained over the NSR, saw the GNR serve the heart of the LNWR empire at Stafford. Back in Nottinghamshire there were also GNR branches to Heanor (opened 1891) and Pinxton (opened 1876).

At the northern end of its line, the GNR boasted a significant network of lines in the West Riding of Yorkshire. The company's terminus in Leeds was Central station, which it shared ultimately with the L&YR. Although there was a GN presence in the area before the route's completion, the GN's main line between Leeds and Doncaster was opened between Leeds and Wakefield on 5 October 1857 (under the auspices of the Bradford, Wakefield & Leeds Railway) and then from Wakefield to Doncaster on 1 February 1866 (with the opening of the West Riding & Grimsby Railway). Prior to this date the GNR's line from Leeds to Bradford Adolphus Street had opened (1854); this terminus would be replaced 13 years later by Exchange, again a joint station with the L&YR. Other GNR lines in the area included Laisterdyke-Ardsley (1856/57), Wrenthorpe-Batley (1862-64), Adwalton-Batley (1863/64), Laisterdyke-Shipley (1874/75), Stanningley-Pudsey Greenside (1877/78), Bradford-Halifax-Queensbury (1876-1884), Pudsey Greenside-Laisterdyke (1893), Dudley Hill-Low Moor (1893/94) and Beeston-Hunslet (1899). The section into Halifax, along with the Halifax High Level line, was jointly owned by the L&YR under the auspices of the Halifax & Ovenden Joint.

One final major part of the GNR network needs to be mentioned — that of the Great Northern & Great Eastern Joint Committee. This was established in 1879 and incorporated the GNR owned lines from Lincoln to Doncaster and from March to Spalding. It formed a link between Doncaster and Huntingdon via St Ives, March, Spalding and Lincoln. One section of new line was constructed for the Joint Committee — that between Spalding and Lincoln which opened in July and August 1882.

The bulk of the GNR network passed intact to the British Railways in 1948, but there had been a number of casualties between 1923 and Nationalisation. For example, the Ramsey North branch had lost its passenger services, as did some of the ex-GNR lines in Nottinghamshire as the LNER rationalised its competing services in the region. In addition, part of the London suburban network had been transferred to the London Passenger Transport Board to facilitate the extension of the Northern Line. The major casualties, however, occurred post 1948. The GN&LNWR network lost its passenger services in the early 1950s, although Leicester Belgrave Road continued to have a curious afterlife of workers' and holidaymakers' trains for a period thereafter. The Queensbury triangle routes lost their passenger services in 1955. The following decade was to witness an almost relentless decline in the fortunes of the ex-GNR network with the closure of the Derby line and the elimination of all the lines in the West Riding, with the exception of the Bradford-Leeds-Wakefield-Doncaster route. These closures were followed by the almost complete elimination of the ex-GNR system in Lincolnshire, with the closure of all the lines in the east of the county with the exception of the route from Boston to Skegness.

Today the ex-GNR lines that survive are primarily the East Coast main line, the route from Doncaster to Leeds and Bradford, the line from Peterborough to Spalding (and then over the GN&GE Joint) to Sleaford, Lincoln and Doncaster, and the line from Nottingham to Grantham and thence to Boston and Skegness.

Now: February 1997
The scene here has changed out of all recognition, with the up and down fast lines having been lifted and the flying junction rebuilt. The building in the background on the right survives, but even the church has gone. No 317347 is about to enter Copenhagen Tunnel working on a service from Peterborough. *Brian Morrison*

Finsbury Park Depot

Then: 20 May 1981

Not strictly a comparison with the steam era, but I felt it appropriate to include this pair to show how quickly things change. Finsbury Park, or the 'Park' as it was known, came on line in April 1960 and was the first purpose-built main line diesel depot constructed in the country. It will always be associated with the 'Deltics', of which all the racehorse-named examples were allocated to Finsbury Park in addition to a number of '47s', '31s' and shunters. The impressive line up of 'Deltics' captured here would have been impossible in the days when they were

working the top diagrams on the East Coast main line, as it would have been very unlikely that four would have been on the 'Park' at any one time, but by this date most of their duties had been taken over by InterCity 125s and the type was relegated to working semi-fast duties. From left to right are Nos 55014 *The Duke of Wellington Regiment*, 55015 *Tulyar*, 55012 *Crepello* (then withdrawn) and 55009 *Alycidon*. *Author*

Now: February 1997

The 'Park' closed as a maintenance depot in June 1981, but it continued at a reduced status, mainly for fuelling purposes, until complete closure in October 1983. It then became derelict and was much the worse for the attention of local vandals. Eventually it was demolished. It was impossible to stand in exactly the same spot as the 'Then' photograph, as the photographer would have been facing the door-knocker of the house above the second white van! To illustrate the vast changes, the viewpoint is a couple of hundred yards back to add interest. Yes, that is a lawn growing on the roof of the building on the right; I wonder who cuts it? *Ken Brunt*

Alexandra Palace

Then: Undated
The GNR branch from Highgate to Alexandra Palace opened on 24 May 1873. This view shows the station platform with, on the right, the Alexandra Palace itself.
Ian Allan Library (L&GRP 26855)

Now: 11 February 1997
The line closed to passenger services on 5 July 1954 and was closed completely between Muswell Hill and Alexandra Palace at the same time. There have been proposals over the years to reopen the line and also the closed section from Finsbury Park to Highgate for passenger services as part of an expanded Northern Line, but so far these have come to nothing. As can be seen, most of the original Alexandra Palace survives, although the platform and trackbed of the station have disappeared. The site was initially built on by British Railways to house a laboratory which tested a variety of things from paint to soil samples. The current building is now the Laboratory Spa & Health Club. Thanks must go to Mr Andy Barker, General Manager, for his kind permission to take the photographs. *Ken Brunt*

Now: 11 February 1997
The station building, seen in the 'Then' photograph to the left at the end of the footbridge is now a community centre. *Ken Brunt*

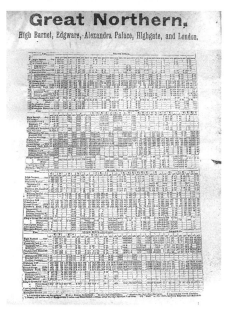

Now: 11 February 1997
On display on the former station is a copy of the original GNR timetable. *Ken Brunt*

Totteridge

Then: 1936
This is the penultimate station on the former GNR branch to High Barnet which was opened on 1 April 1872. This view was taken almost contemporaneously with the scheme that was to lead to the transfer of the line from Highgate to High Barnet from LNER operation to the London Passenger Transport Board as part of the expansion of the Northern Line.
Ian Allan Library (9097)

Oakleigh Park

Then: Undated (1930s)
It is a pleasure to be able to include this fine picture of the up 'Silver Jubilee' racing through the station at around 80mph headed by King's Cross 'A4' No 2512 *Silver Fox* (later BR No 60017). The photographer has done very well to stop the train at this speed and one can clearly see the 'Silver Fox' badge under the painted-on name.
F. R. Hebron

Now: 8 February 1997
Northern Line trains began to operate to East Finchley on 3 July 1939 and on the following 14 April electric trains commenced operation over the High Barnet route. Much of the old station shown in the 'Then' photograph remains, although the signalbox and gas lamps have vanished. A typical rake of Northern Line stock is pictured heading north. *Author*

Now: 27 January 1997
This is quite a comparison; the very latest rolling stock on the East Coast main line, one of West Anglia & Great Northern's new Class 365s, No 365537, heads south forming the 12.07 service from Huntingdon to King's Cross. Although the station footbridge has been rebuilt, the station buildings still survive. *Author*

New Barnet

Then: 1932
Services through New Barnet started on 8 August 1850. The station, which was one of the original stations when the line opened, was rebuilt in 1896. This view, taken prior to World War 2, shows a very tidy station and surrounding area.
Ian Allan Library (9095)

Now: 8 February 1997
Most of the old station buildings and platform roofs have gone, no doubt when the line was electrified (services commencing on 8 November 1976). Class 317 EMU No 317311 heads towards King's Cross with a service that had probably originated at King's Lynn. The station platform and area look a mess in comparison with the condition 65 years ago. *Author*

Hatfield

Then: July 1961

The East Coast main line opened through Hatfield on 8 August 1850 and the station was eventually to become an important junction, with lines running to St Albans (1865), Dunstable (1860) and Hertford (1876); in both the latter two cases the lines had originally been built to serve Welwyn — in 1858 and 1860 respectively — but were extended to Hatfield subsequently, running parallel to the East Coast main line. An up express, headed by King's Cross-allocated 'A4' No 60021 *Wild Swan*, heads south on the up fast line. Note the size of the station awning on the up slow platform compared to the present one. There was a steam shed here until 1961, with an allocation of around 25 0-6-2Ts of Classes N7 and N2. *Ian Allan Library (K4743)*

Now: 8 February 1997

Passenger services over the three branches have succumbed: to Hertford on 18 June 1951; to St Albans on 1 October 1951; and to Dunstable on 26 April 1965. The final section of the St Albans route, between Hatfield and Butterwick, closed completely on 1 January 1969. Freight has also been withdrawn from both the Dunstable and Hertford lines leaving Hatfield served only by services over the ECML. The 07.00 Glasgow Central-King's Cross service, in the new GNER livery, passes through the station on the up fast line. The staggered platforms are still in existence, but the fine station building has now been replaced with a modern structure. *Author*

Harpenden East

Then: 14 June 1962
The GNR branch from Hatfield to Dunstable opened on 1 September 1860. Via a connection with the LNWR it provided the GNR with a link to the West Coast main line at Leighton Buzzard. Privately owned ex-GNR Class J52 0-6-0T No 1247 (BR No 68846) was used by the Stephenson Locomotive Society for a special from Hatfield. The train paused for a photographic stop *en route* to Luton. The train had originated from Birmingham New Street and utilised LMS Class 2P 4-4-0 No 40646 for most of the tour. *Author*

Now: 8 February 1997
The line between Hatfield and Leighton Buzzard lost its passenger services in two stages: from Dunstable to Leighton Buzzard on 2 July 1962 and from Hatfield, via Harpenden East, to Dunstable on 26 April 1965. In 1966 a link was established in Luton between the ex-Midland route and the ex-GNR line to Dunstable, allowing complete closure of the line from Hatfield. All signs of the railway have vanished and, as can be seen, the former station site is now in the middle of a housing estate. *Author*

Luton Bute Street

Then: Undated
Opened on 1 September 1860 on the GNR branch from Hatfield to Dunstable, this station was alongside the Midland station and the signals of the Midland main line are just visible in the background.
J. Spencer Gilks

Welwyn Garden City

Then: June 1951
Although the line from Peterborough to London King's Cross opened on 8 August 1850, it was not until 20 September 1926 that a station was built to serve Welwyn Garden City. An 'N7' 0-6-2T, believed to be No 69699, is shown in what is today the up slow platform. Over on the down slow line is a rake of suburban stock formed in part with an articulated rake. The fast lines pass through the centre roads on the right.
Ian Allan Library (K1139)

Sleaford

Then: 29 August 1964
This important railway location is the point where the Nottingham-Boston route meets the Great Northern & Great Eastern Joint line (which opened from Spalding to a point north of Sleaford on 6 March 1882). The main GN&GE line bypassed the station, but a loop was also built to allow access to the station. In addition, Sleaford was served by trains on the GNR route from Essendine and Bourne (which closed to passenger services between Bourne and Sleaford on 22 September 1930 and to freight south of Sleaford to Billingborough on 28 July 1956). The train portrayed is a summer special from Derby to Mablethorpe and is headed by a very dirty Class B1 4-6-0 No 61141. *R. Madley*

Now: 8 February 1997
Passenger services over the GNR Hatfield-Dunstable line were withdrawn on 26 April 1965. The line remained open, however, to serve the various parts of the vast General Motors operation in Luton and Dunstable. In 1966 a link between the Midland and GN routes was opened. The line was, however, mothballed on 30 April 1989 and a short section of track has subsequently been lifted in Luton. There have been proposals for reopening the line to Dunstable, but nothing has as yet resulted. The electrified Midland main line can be seen in the background, whilst the old station site has become a large car park. This is no doubt well used by commuters to London. *Author*

Now: 8 February 1997
EMU No 317317 pauses in the station with an up train for King's Cross. The footbridge has been rebuilt over the station, but remains unchanged over the site of the goods yard on the left. A new shopping centre has opened on the west side of the station and one of the station entrances is now through the complex. *Author*

Now: 24 September 1996
The railways around Sleaford are still in use, although many of the sidings have been removed. It is a connecting point for trains from Lincoln down to Peterborough with those on the cross-country service from Skegness to Nottingham and beyond. Class 153 No 153306 is shown arriving with the 17.31 departure for Skegness. *Author*

Spalding

Then: September 1960

The GNR route from Peterborough to Boston via Spalding opened on 17 October 1848. The town was to become an important centre with lines radiating to Sleaford (GN&GE Joint; opened 6 March 1882), March (GN&GE Joint; 1 April 1867), Bourne (M&GN; opened 1 May 1866) and Sutton Bridge (M&GN). A considerable quantity of freight traffic passed through the town heading south to London, via Whitemoor Yard, and Peterborough. The large station was especially busy during the spring with the annual Tulip Festival. A dirty York-based Class B16 No 61422 heads south with an up freight bound for Whitemoor Yard. *John C. Baker*

Now: 14 November 1996

Spalding's importance has declined over recent years, and even the annual flower festival rarely brings special traffic today. Passenger traffic over the M&GN routes ceased on 2 March 1959 and the original GNR line from Peterborough to Boston lost its passenger services on 5 October 1970; the latter were, however, reinstated between Peterborough and Spalding on 7 June 1971. Passenger services over the route south to March were withdrawn on 28 November 1982 and the section between Whitemoor Yard and Spalding was closed completely at the same time. As can be seen, although the bridge across the closed platforms still stands as do some of the station buildings, Spalding is very much a shadow of its former glory. A service operates between Peterborough and Lincoln, with occasional through services to Doncaster. *Author*

Boston

Then: 13 August 1965
The Great Northern first reached Boston on 1 October 1848 when the line from Firsby was opened. The town's railway network soon expanded to include links with Peterborough, Lincoln and Sleaford. A considerable amount of traffic was also generated by the town's harbour. The town could lay claim to a locomotive shed (coded 40F), which housed many Class J6 0-6-0s and 'K2' 2-6-0s and which closed in 1964. Here Class B1 4-6-0 No 61210 arrives with a M-FO summer train from Nottingham Midland to Mablethorpe. *J. Cupit*

Now: 24 September 1996
Today, although requirements have been reduced by the decline in passenger services to the Sleaford-Skegness corridor alone following the closures of October 1970, the main station building has been restored and looks very impressive. However, as is apparent in this view taken from the footbridge, little remains of the earlier track layout except the two through running lines. West Street Junction signalbox still survives. The services are mainly now in the hands of Classes 156 and 153. No 156412 with No 153383 at the rear arrives with the 13.16 from Crewe. These services now usually originate at Crewe and travel via Nottingham. *Author*

Skegness

Then: 8 September 1963
The line to Skegness was opened between Wainfleet — which the railways had reached in November 1871 — and the town on 28 July 1873. Since the arrival of the railways, the town has become and remains a popular east coast holiday resort and in the pre- and postwar years people flocked to the town in huge numbers. A busy scene is depicted in this photograph, showing from left to right Class B1 4-6-0s Nos 61070, 61122, 61141 and 61264. The last mentioned was to be rescued for preservation and is now restored.
M. Mitchell

Spilsby

Then: 1950
The short branch from Firsby Junction to Spilsby had no intermediate stations. It was opened on 1 May 1868. Passenger services over the branch were suspended on 11 September 1939 and were never reintroduced. Thus by the date of this photograph the branch had been reduced to freight-only operation.
Ian Allan Library (23514)

Now: 24 September 1996
Freight services continued until withdrawal on 1 December 1958. My thanks must go to the manager of Chandler Farm Equipment Ltd for allowing me into their premises to take this picture. As you can see, there is little to remind you that this was once a branch line terminus. *Author*

Now: 24 September 1996
Although traffic has declined, even in the 1980s there were several summer Saturday specials run every weekend, but there are currently fewer of these extras. The tracks into all the platforms are still intact, as are the signals and the signalbox. The goods sidings on the far right of the picture are now removed. There is far more space available than is required for the basically hourly service of two-car Class 156 units to Nottingham and beyond. Unit No 156403 is shown ready to leave with the 15.18 departure for Crewe. A supermarket to the left of the picture is now built on what used to be railway property. *Author*

Horncastle

Then: 16 May 1954
The branch from Woodhall Junction to Horncastle in Lincolnshire served only one intermediate station (Woodhall Spa) and was opened on 11 August 1855. Constructed by the Horncastle Railway, it was operated from the start by the GNR. Class J6 0-6-0 No 64199 is seen at the terminus with a Railway Correspondence & Travel Society special.
Ian Allan Library (K2230)

Now: 24 September 1996
Passenger services over the branch succumbed shortly after the date of the special, on 13 September 1954. Freight was to last until 5 April 1971. I have selected a slightly higher viewpoint than in the 'Then' photograph to show that the platform still exists. New houses were being built to the left of the site and it appeared that the rest would be developed very shortly. *Author*

Louth

Then: 29 June 1977
It was from Louth to Grimsby on 1 March 1848 that the GNR operated its first trains in the region. Services were extended southwards to Firsby on 3 September 1848. Louth was destined to become an important junction with the line to Bardney opening on 1 December 1876 and that to Mablethorpe following on 17 October 1877. Passenger services over the Bardney line were withdrawn on 5 November 1951 and freight was withdrawn over the route progressively until it was closed completely in 1956. The route to Mablethorpe was closed completely with the withdrawal of passenger services on 5 December 1960. Louth was to lose its passenger services completely on 5 October 1970 with the wholesale withdrawal of services over much of the ex-GNR network in east Lincolnshire. At the same time, the line south to Firsby was closed completely, leaving Louth to be served as a freight terminus from Grimsby. This was the state of the station, with a single track passing through. *S. Creer*

Lincoln Central

Then: 20 June 1960
Great Northern services first reached Lincoln on 17 October 1848 and the city developed into an important railway centre, with services provided by the Great Central and Midland railways as well as those over the GN&GE Joint and GN lines. Gresley Class V2 2-6-2 No 60948, which at the time was allocated to March (31B), arrives at the station from the north with a train for Colchester. Lincoln also had a second station, St Marks, which was used by Midland trains. The steam shed at Lincoln was coded 40A and in 1950 had an allocation of 64 locomotives; it closed in 1964. *D. C. Ovenden*

Bardney

Then: 16 May 1954
This town is about 12 miles east of Lincoln and was the point at which the ex-GNR routes divided, one going northeastwards towards Louth (which opened on 1 December 1876) whilst the main line continued towards Boston. The Boston-Lincoln route had opened on 17 October 1848. By the date of this photograph, passenger services had already been withdrawn from the Louth line (5 November 1951). The picture shows a Class J6 0-6-0 No 64199 heading an RCTS special to the area. *Ian Allan Library (K2222)*

Now: 9 November 1996
The freight-only operation came to an end on 7 October 1980 and the track was subsequently lifted. A preservation scheme currently is endeavouring to reopen the line. The attractive station has recently become flats and a superb job has been done in converting the building. The trackbed has been made into a lawn. Further development has also taken place around the station. The level crossing and signalbox still exist at the north end of the station. Louth is now in the middle of a large area of Lincolnshire that is completely devoid of railways. *Author*

Now: 24 September 1996
As will be seen from this picture, the location has changed very little. The footbridge has gone and a multistorey building has appeared in the background. The level crossing at the east end, which caused so much traffic chaos, has been replaced by a bridge, but the traffic in the city centre is still very heavy. With the closure of St Marks station, all services have been concentrated on Central. Centro-liveried Class 150/1 No 150127 has just arrived prior to forming the 12.41 departure for Grimsby. Elsewhere, however, the story in Lincoln is not so good, with virtually all the railway infrastructure having vanished; even the depot built to service the area's DMU fleet has closed. *Author*

Now: 24 September 1996
The Louth line was progressively closed up to 1956. The main Lincoln-Boston route retained passenger services until 5 October 1970. Apart from the section from Lincoln to serve the British Sugar works at Bardney (visible in the background here), the lines closed completely at that time. The section to serve the sugar works lasted until the 1980s, but has subsequently closed. There are still signs that the railway existed here, but these are behind the photographer. *Author*

Huntingdon

Then: 16 October 1976
Although this 'Then' photograph was taken only 20 years ago, there have been big changes at this location. The GNR line between Peterborough and London opened for services on 7 August 1850. A Class 47/4, No 47527, passes on the down fast line at the head of the 16.00 King's Cross-Edinburgh Waverley express, whilst a Class 105 DMU is ready to leave with a Peterborough local service. *Author*

Ramsey North

Then: 1952
There were two stations at Ramsey, North being that of the GNR whilst East was served by the GN&GE Joint line from a junction at Somersham. The two stations were less than a mile apart but, being situated on either side of the small town, were never connected. The line from Holme on the GNR to Ramsey, which ran for 5½ miles, was opened on 22 July 1863; the line from Somersham opened on 16 September 1889. Passenger services over the route from Somersham ceased on 22 September 1930 (with freight being withdrawn over the section north of Warboys in August 1957), whilst passenger services from Holme succumbed on 6 October 1947. *Ian Allan Library*

Sandy

Then: March 1963
A powerful picture of a King's Cross-allocated Gresley 'A3' Pacific storming through the station as it heads an up Leeds-King's Cross express. The locomotive, No 60110 *Robert the Devil* is not in the external condition normally expected of 'Top Shed', but the locomotive was only two months from withdrawal. 'Top Shed' was also to close in 1963. The ex-LNWR line from Bedford to Cambridge crossed the ECML to the north of the station and the platforms for these trains can be seen on the right of the picture. *I. J. Hodson*

Now: 8 February 1997
In sharp contrast to the Class A3, the DVT-headed express glided almost silently past at around 120mph on an up working. The island platform has gone, and Sandy is now served by trains only on the up and down slow lines. A new footbridge has also been installed, as has a new road bridge. The ex-LNWR route between Bedford and Cambridge was closed completely on 1 January 1968. *Author*

Now: 18 January 1997
The old island platform has been moved over to serve only the local services, whilst the yard has been converted into a car park. The route has been electrified, and the station is now very much part of the London commuter operation. Class 317 EMU No 317312 has just arrived with the 12.16 service from Peterborough to King's Cross. *Author*

Now: 18 January 1997
Freight continued to serve the Ramsey North branch until 2 July 1973. When I visited the site of station and yard for this photograph, it was derelict, the only link between the two pictures being the houses on the right-hand side. *Author*

Abbots Ripton

Then: Undated
An undated photograph shows a Class B1 4-6-0, No 61091, heading north along the East Coast main line at Abbots Ripton. The section of the ECML between Peterborough and London opened on 7 August 1850. *Eric Treacy*

Now: 18 January 1997
The crossover and the up slow line have gone but, apart from the electrification, this location has not altered a lot. However, just look how tidy the embankment was in the 1950s in comparison with the present scene. A Class 91 with a rake of coaches, newly repainted into the GNER livery of the privatised Train Operating Company, heads north at around 120mph on the 10.10 King's Cross-Leeds train. Needless to say, I did not get the number! *Author*

Peterborough station (north end)

Then: March 1961
The first stretch of the GNR to open in Peterborough was the route to Boston, which opened on 17 October 1848. This was followed on 7 August 1850 by the completion of the main line south to London. Finally, the section north through Grantham was opened on 15 July 1852 for freight and the following 1 August for passenger traffic. This station was also served by M&GNJR trains from Sutton Bridge. The complex layout around Peterborough station, which became such a bottleneck on the East Coast main line, is shown to advantage in this picture of a Class B1 4-6-0 No 61364 heading north on an empty coal train. In the background can be seen an 'A4' Pacific, no doubt getting ready to take over an express to King's Cross. *G. D. King*

Now: 18 January 1997
The 'Now' photograph makes an interesting comparison to show how the tracks have been rationalised and straightened out to allow for high-speed running through the station. Unfortunately, the fine viewing points from the bridge have now been ruined by the electrification, as is clear in this photograph of Class 91 No 91028 *Guide Dog* leaving on the 12.30 King's Cross-Leeds service. To the left are two Class 31s, the one nearest the camera being the unique Mainline-liveried member of the class, No 31407. *Author*

Peterborough North

Then: Undated
A Class B1 4-6-0 No 61390 is shown approaching Peterborough from the north on a semi-fast train. On the skyline above the bridge can be seen the area which was at that time occupied by New England shed, which was to close in January 1965. In the early 1950s New England had an allocation of over 200 locomotives. The tracks on the left were those used by the ex-Midland Railway route from Stamford and by the ex-M&GN route from Sutton Bridge. The latter crossed over the East Coast main line on a bridge just to the north of New England shed. *J. Davenport*

Now: 18 January 1997
Although the track layout has been rationalised, there is much that is still similar. The ex-Midland line survives, although the ex-M&GN route is now long closed and dismantled. The current locomotive servicing point is now to the right of the picture and on this occasion Class 58s Nos 58025 and 58015 were present together with others. Class 158 unit No 158795 is shown leaving on the 11.50 Norwich-Liverpool service. It was due to arrive on Merseyside at 17.29. *Author*

Essendine

Then: 11 October 1958
This was the main station between Peterborough and Grantham, and was the junction for the lines to Bourne (opened 16 June 1860; closed completely with the withdrawal of passenger services on 18 June 1951) and Stamford (opened 1 November 1856). The GNR main line reached here in 1852 and the location became well known as being the place where the maximum speeds of trains coming down Stoke Bank used to be reached. As can be seen in the picture, it was quite a busy place. King's Cross-allocated 'A4' No 60007 *Sir Nigel Gresley* is leaving on the 1.30pm service to Grantham. Also in the picture is Class C12 4-4-2T No 67398, which has just detached itself from the single coach for the Stamford train and is waiting to return to New England shed at Peterborough after two weeks' service on the branch. Class N5 0-6-2T No 69293 took over the service on this occasion. *P. H. Wells*

Now: 15 October 1996
The branch to Stamford closed completely on 15 June 1959 with the withdrawal of passenger services, and the station at Essendine closed at the same time; freight was handled at the station until 7 March 1966. Today there are only the four running lines and the Class 91 electrics go up Stoke Bank as fast as they descend it. As can be seen, there is little evidence that a station once existed here. Class 91 No 91021 *Royal Armouries* is pictured heading north on the 14.10 service to Leeds. *Author*

Stamford East

Then: October 1954
This was the terminus of a short branch from Essendine, which opened on 1 November 1856. Stamford was also served by the Midland Railway and there was a connection between the two. The station is famous for its very ornate and impressive frontage, the result of the patronage of the Marquis of Exeter. Class C12 4-4-2T No 67389, typical of a class familiar on this service for many years, is shown ready to depart for its journey to Essendine. *Ian Allan Library (K2418)*

Now: 15 October 1996
Trains ceased to terminate at Stamford East on 4 March 1957, being transferred to run from the ex-Midland station until the service was withdrawn on 15 June 1959 at which time the ex-GNR line was close completely. As can be seen, the changes are dramatic. These flats/houses have been built and the area has been developed into a very pleasant spot. It was not possible to gain access to the position from where the 'Then' photograph had been taken, which was on the north side of the station, so I took this view from the south side, which I believe was about where the building behind the station sign in the earlier photograph is situated, to illustrate what had happened in the area. *Author*

Great Ponton

Then: 2 August 1958
This station was located to the north of Stoke Summit on the East Coast main line to Grantham. At the date of the photograph the English Electric Type 4 (later Class 40) No D206 was less than one month old. It is seen at the head of an up express climbing the 1 in 200 gradient towards Stoke Summit from Grantham. *Author*

Now: 15 October 1996
Great Ponton station closed on 15 September 1958 and freight facilities were withdrawn on 29 April 1963. Today there are no signs of the platforms and the trees have grown considerably, giving this very limited view of the now electrified East Coast main line. *Author*

Grantham South

Then: 5 August 1962

Opened to freight on 15 July 1852 and to passengers on the following 1 August, the stretch of the GNR main line through Grantham was the last part of the route between London and Doncaster to be completed. Grantham was where many of the steam-hauled expresses changed locomotives. This view, which must have been taken from a convenient signal, shows the 10.25am Sunderland-King's Cross service having its motive power changed with local Class A3 No 60047 *Donovan* about to take over from King's Cross 'A4' No 60025 *Falcon*. An 'L1' class 2-6-4T can be seen in the sidings to the left after probably working a local from Nottingham, and the shed (which closed in 1963) is out of sight to the left of the picture. *J. M. Rayner*

Now: 15 October 1996

This telephoto shot taken from the old Great North Road bridge, about 400yd further south than the 'Then' shot, shows what little there is left at Grantham. The 12.00 from Glasgow to King's Cross is shown passing as it heads south. *Author*

Grantham

Then: 31 July 1953
The Great Northern arrived at Grantham in 1852 and the town developed into an important railway centre, where the lines to Nottingham and to Skegness (from Barkston Junction) left the main line. It was also the point where many of the expresses changed locomotives, having worked through from either King's Cross or from the north. The town had a locomotive shed, coded 35B with an allocation of Pacifics, and in 1959 there were 41 locomotives allocated; it was, however, to close in 1963. The coaling plant can just be seen above the 'V2' in this fine picture. Also visible is a fantastic variety of motive power: 'B12' 4-6-0 No 61538 is in the bay with a Derby local train; 'B1' 4-6-0 No 61207 is on a train for Skegness; and 'V2' 2-6-2 No 60961 waits to take over a down express. In the background is 'A4' Pacific No 60007 *Sir Nigel Gresley. H. W. Hayle*

Bottesford

Then: 9 August 1962
Bottesford station is located about seven miles west of Grantham on the line towards Nottingham, which was opened on 15 July 1850. It was an important centre, with lines also heading north to Newark and south on to the GN&LNWR Joint line, over which the GNR gained access to Leicester. The route at one time carried a considerable amount of freight from the East Midlands, heading across country towards Sleaford and thence over the GN&GE Joint line to Whitemoor Yard at March. Class L1 2-6-4T No 67745, showing a 40E shed plate (Colwick), pauses at the station with the 4.18pm Grantham-Derby local service. *J. M. Rayner*

Lowesby

Then: 27 August 1960
There used to be a triangular junction at Lowesby between the ex-GNR line heading east out of Leicester Belgrave Road and the GN&LNWR Joint line between Melton Mowbray and Hallaton. Lowesby station was on the route into Leicester Belgrave Road which opened on 1 January 1883. Passenger services over the route were withdrawn on 7 December 1953, except for workmen's services (which were withdrawn on 29 April 1957) and excursion traffic to Skegness and Mablethorpe. One of these excursion trains returning from Mablethorpe is seen passing through the station behind 'B1' 4-6-0 No 61390; the weeds are already well established both on the track and on the platforms.
J. Spencer Gilks

Now: 18 January 1997
The station is now on the outer limits of London commuter land, with the InterCity 125s and Class 91-hauled services taking only about an hour for the 105-mile journey, but the atmosphere has gone from the refurbished station. Class 158 No 158862 arrives on the 11.52 from Liverpool Lime Street to Norwich. It was due to depart from Grantham at 15.06. *Author*

Now: 15 October 1996
Today there is still a roughly half-hourly service between Nottingham and Grantham, with Crewe-Skegness trains normally passing through the station non-stop. They are usually Class 156 Sprinters or single-unit Class 153s. Here No 153321 is pictured heading east on the 09.30 service from Derby to Skegness. *Author*

Now: 15 October 1996
The final excursion trains operated in the summer of 1962; thereafter the line remained open for freight access to Belgrave Road. With the opening of a link to the ex-MR route at Humberstone on 1 June 1964, the line eastwards from that point was closed completely. Leicester Belgrave Road was to close finally on 2 June 1969. When I visited the site, the yard was being used by a local coal merchant and the station buildings, although still standing, were in a sorry state. The platforms are still *in situ*. *Author*

Great Dalby

Then: 25 June 1960

This station, situated between Lowesby and Melton Mowbray on the GN&LNWR Joint line, was opened on 15 December 1879. The section of line north from Melton Mowbray opened on 30 June 1879 and the final piece, the Belgrave Road branch, opened on 1 January 1883. Passenger services between Bottesford and Market Harborough and over the line to Leicester Belgrave Road were withdrawn on 7 December 1953. Freight, however, continued to use the GN&LNWR Joint routes thereafter, and some excursion traffic continued to operate out of Leicester Belgrave Road to Mablethorpe and Skegness. Class B1 4-6-0 No 61163 is pictured heading the 12-coach 1.20pm Saturdays Only service from Skegness to Belgrave Road through the station. As with Lowesby, the weeds have taken over on the station platforms. *M. Mitchell*

Now: 15 October 1996

The final excursion traffic operated over the route in the summer of 1962 and on 1 June 1964 the route was closed completely when a new connection at Humberstone, near Leicester, to the Midland route allowed the freight terminal at Belgrave Road to be served by an alternative route. Today there is little to indicate that a railway passed through here, although hidden in the trees in the background is the bridge over the road. *Author*

East Norton

Then: 2 August 1962
This station was situated on the GN&LNWR Joint line south of the triangular junction at Lowesby. The section south from Melton Mowbray to Welham opened on 15 December 1879. Passenger services over the route were withdrawn on 7 December 1953, but the line remained an important freight route. Here 'Austerity' 2-8-0 No 90717 is caught at the head of the 8am freight from Welham Junction to Melton Mowbray (North). The picture was taken from the high road bridge on what is now the busy A47 from Leicester to Peterborough. *P. H. Wells*

Now: 15 October 1996
Freight services over the Marefield Junction-Welham Junction section were withdrawn on 4 November 1963. I found it hard to believe that this was the same location, although the station still exists and is occupied; it is to the right of this photograph. The viaduct can just be seen to the left of the pole in the upper centre; in the 'Then' photograph it is hidden behind the platform building's chimney. I assume that there was a massive landfill operation when the A47 was upgraded; whatever the reason, the change is dramatic. *Author*

Kimberley East

Then: 1952
This station was situated on the Great Northern line which headed west after branching off from the GNR line north from Nottingham. Passenger services between Nottingham and Pinxton were introduced on 1 August 1876.
Ian Allan Library (26295)

Ilkeston North

Then: 1952
This was the GNR station in the town, Ilkeston Town being the Midland Railway station. Passenger services over the route from Kimberley East to Derby Friargate opened on 1 April 1878. Ilkeston was the junction for the passenger line to Heanor (which opened on 1 July 1891 as an extension of the freight branch to Shipley opened in June 1885), which lost its passenger services on 4 December 1939. There was also a freight-only branch south to Stanton. *Ian Allan Library (26277)*

Now: 11 August 1996
Passenger services over the Pinxton-Kimberley East section were withdrawn on 7 January 1963 leaving the station to be served by trains over the Derby Friargate-Nottingham Victoria route. These were in turn to be withdrawn on 7 September 1964. Freight facilities ended two months later. The trackbed has now been converted into a nature walk and there are plaques giving some information on its past uses, one of which says that in the 1950s 160 trains per day used the lines, a fact which stretches the imagination a bit when looking at the current scene. *Author*

Hucknall Town

Then: 1952
The corridor running north from Nottingham was well served by railways, with the Midland, Great Central and Great Northern railways all competing for the traffic in the district. The GNR route to Newstead opened on 2 October 1882 and thence to Shirebrook on 1 November 1901. Following the Grouping in 1923, the LNER rationalised its passenger services through the region in 1931 when all services were routed over the ex-GC line. More than 20 years after closure, the ex-GNR station still looks in a remarkable state of preservation. *Ian Allan Library (26280)*

Now: 29 November 1996
The station retained goods facilities until 5 April 1965. There are still signs of the railway on the other side of the hospital which now occupies the station and railway yard. *Author*

Now: 12 October 1996
Passenger services over the Derby Friargate-Nottingham line on 7 September 1964; freight had already been withdrawn on the Heanor line (7 October 1963) and the Stanton line (on 2 December 1963). Complete closure of the main route through Ilkeston came on 3 June 1968. Everything has vanished here with the exception of the top of the road bridge, which passed behind the station when looking east. *Author*

Egginton Junction

Then: 1957
It was at Egginton Junction that the GNR met the North Staffordshire Railway's route from Stoke to Derby. Over this line the GNR gained access to its isolated section from Bromshall to Stafford. Passenger services over the GNR route from Kimberley to Egginton were introduced on 1 April 1878. However, they were withdrawn on 4 December 1939 on the section from Derby Friargate to Egginton. The section was retained for freight traffic.
Ian Allan Library (25525)

Tuxford North

Then: 1950
The GNR main line through Grantham to Retford opened in 1852. This picture was probably taken from the old level crossing, just to the north of the station, which was closed a number of years ago and replaced by a bridge. There were two stations at Tuxford; the other was situated on the GCR line from Lincoln westwards to Edwinstowe. There was also a steam shed here, originally coded 40D and then 41K.
Ian Allan Library (23549)

Derby Friargate

Then: Undated
Passenger services between Kimberley East and Egginton Junction were introduced on 1 April 1878 and were withdrawn between Egginton Junction and Derby Friargate on 4 December 1939. Neither the 'Then' or 'Now' photograph gives the impression that the station was situated nearly in the centre of Derby. This undated photograph shows a great deal of activity in the station.
Ian Allan Library

Now: 11 August 1996
Passenger services from Derby Friargate to Nottingham were withdrawn on 7 September 1964. The section north of Derby Friargate closed completely on 4 September 1967. The section south of Derby was, however, retained as a test track for use by the Derby-based RTC. The section between Mickleover and Derby Friargate closed completely on 26 November 1971. Despite its proximity to the city centre, the site of Derby Friargate is, as can be seen, undeveloped. *Author*

Now: 11 August 1996
After the closure of the line north from Derby Friargate in 1967, the section from Egginton to Derby was retained as a test track. It was abandoned north of Mickleover in November 1971, but survived between Egginton and Mickleover until the last train operated over it on 9 July 1990. The North Staffordshire line still runs, providing a link in the Crewe-Derby service. The track to Mickleover — a location which was used to store withdrawn locomotives, several Class 45s spending time dumped there — has recently been lifted. The station has now become the headquarters of the National Federation of Anglers; the building is beautifully restored and set in impressive grounds. *Author*

Now: 15 October 1996
Tuxford North station closed on 4 July 1955. The steam shed closed in 1959 and the site lost its freight facilities on 15 June 1964. This picture was taken from the middle of the new road bridge, giving an elevated view of the line and the business to the right of the line, which exports old diesel engines salvaged from lorries.
Author

Retford

Then: May 1961

The GNR opened its route from Retford north to Doncaster on
4 September 1849. Access to the line was gained via Lincoln and the
Sykes Junction-Retford route (later part of the GCR). The through route
south of Retford opened on 15 July 1852. Retford developed into an
important centre, because it was here that the GNR crossed the GCR
line from Sheffield to Lincoln on a flat crossing, as shown in this picture
of Class A1 No 60144 *King's Courier* heading a down express. There
was a locomotive shed here, coded 36E, which in 1959 had an
allocation of 59 locomotives, but had been reduced to 35 by the time it
closed in 1965. There were two buildings at the shed, one of GN and the
other of GC origin, but it was considered as one facility. *J. C. Baker*

Now: 11 February 1997

The flat crossing at Retford was always a problem for operation of the
East Coast main line, and in the mid-1960s it was replaced with a new
formation which saw the ex-GCR line pass under the ECML. The ex-
GCR lines are served by two new platforms alongside the new
alignment. As can be seen, the track formation at this location is very
much simplified. Class 91 No 91006, with a complete rake of GNER-
liveried stock, rushes through on the down 10.00 service from King's
Cross to Glasgow. *Author*

Doncaster South

Then: 31 August 1961

Doncaster was really the centre of the Great Northern Railway, where the famous Atlantics and Pacifics were built at the 'Plant'. The ex-GNR works are out of sight to the left in this photograph. It was on 6 June 1848 that the section between Askern Junction and Arksey (just to the north of Doncaster) was opened; this was extended into Doncaster itself on 7 September the same year. On 4 September 1849 the line south to Retford was opened. Doncaster was eventually to become one of the country's major railway centres, served by a complex network of lines. A sight familiar for many years was the standby locomotive, which, on this occasion, was a local 'A1' Pacific. The up 'Elizabethan', headed by one of Edinburgh's favourite Haymarket-based 'A4' Pacifics, No 60009 *Union of South Africa*, had no need of its services as it headed south. *Author*

Now: 11 October 1996

Rationalisation of the track has taken place around the station and in the immediate area. The standby locomotive is still on duty, but this was now a Res-liveried Class 47 No 47474 *Sir Rowland Hill* — which incidentally was the first to receive the red livery. One of the National Power coal trains passes through loaded for either Drax or Eggborough power station; it has probably originated from Maltby colliery. In the distance a Class 158 approaches the platform with a service from Sheffield to Cleethorpes. *Author*

Gainsborough Lea Road

Then: June 1952
The Great Northern Railway first reached Gainsborough from Lincoln on 9 April 1848. The town was eventually to become a significant junction with lines to Barnetby (opened 2 April 1850), Doncaster (opened 15 July 1867) and Retford (opened 17 July 1849). Although built by the GNR, control of the line from Lincoln to Doncaster passed to the control of the GN&GE Joint when that was established in 1882. Doncaster-based Gresley Class K3 2-6-0 No 61861 is seen arriving with a westbound train. *Ian Allan Library*

South Elmsall

Then: 24 August 1961
Located on the West Riding & Grimsby Joint line — controlled by the GNR and MS&LR — the route between Wakefield Westgate and Doncaster opened on 1 February 1866. Pacific No 60153 *Flamboyant* is seen arriving with a stopping train for Leeds. This was the one roller-bearing fitted Class A1 allocated to York and was one of three members of the class never to be transferred to another shed, the others being Nos 60121 and 60138, which were also York engines. *Author*

Beeston Junction

Then: 5 June 1962

Situated on the south side of Leeds, it this was always a favourite location to take photographs of the King's Cross trains. On this occasion one of the famous King's Cross 'A4s', No 60033 *Seagull*, heads south past the signalbox with the 10am from Leeds Central. Curving off to the right in the background is the line that used to head towards Hunslet and eventually Neville Hill. This freight-only line was opened from Beeston Junction to Hunslet on 3 July 1899. At Hunslet it connected with the NER line from Neville Hill opened on 2 January the same year. Slightly to the south of Beeston Junction, the line to Batley via Tingley left the main line, but this had closed on 6 July 1953. *Author*

Now: 5 February 1997

The line to Hunslet closed between Beeston Junction and Parkside Junction on 3 July 1967. Only the two through lines now remain and another once fine photographic location has vanished amidst the trees and wires. Here Pacer unit No 144087 passes on the 13.15 Leeds-Sheffield service. Although it does not appear in the photograph, the land to the left has now been developed and yet another big shopping centre has been built. *Author*

Beeston

Then: 6 June 1962
The station here opened in February 1860, some two years after the line had opened between Leeds and Wakefield. It closed on 2 March 1953, but the station nameboards were still in place almost a decade later as 'B1' 4-6-0 No 61320 headed a Leeds-Doncaster local past the disused platforms. Note the articulated coaches in the formation. *Author*

Now: 5 February 1997
The old platforms have now vanished, although on the down side some evidence of their existence still survives. The 13.05 from Leeds to King's Cross passes headed by a DVT and with Class 91 No 91014 *Northern Electric* at the rear. The area now has a considerable amount of industry, plus the new shopping centre and residential development. The possibility of reopening the station has been discussed for a number of years, but as yet nothing has happened. *Author*

Wortley Junction, South

Then: 6 August 1965

This location is situated on the south side of the triangle that used to surround Copley Hill locomotive shed and carriage sidings. The lines from Wortley East Junction to Ings Road Junction in Wakefield and from Wortley West to Wortley South junctions were both opened on 5 October 1857. Holbeck-allocated Stanier Class 5 No 44857 heads the 4.50pm stopping train from Leeds to Doncaster. On the right-hand side can be seen the extensive LNWR goods yard together with the Leeds-Huddersfield main line via Whitehall Junction. The lines in the foreground are those to Bradford Exchange which, at this time, were used by express services between Bradford and King's Cross or, earlier, by the Bradford portions of through expresses. This was an excellent point to observe the services over the ex-GN and ex-LNWR lines into Leeds. *Author*

Now: 5 February 1997

After much controversy — particularly from Bradford which feared the move presaged the end of through services between the city and London — the Wortley South-Wortley West line was severed at this point in 1984. The track still remains, but is not connected to the main line from Wakefield. InterCity 125 power car No 43088 heads the 13.38 Newcastle-Bristol service round the curve. The view is now very restricted by bushes, and the ex-LNWR goods yard is full of industrial units. *Author*

Copley Hill

Then: 29 August 1961

I suppose in preparing a book of this format that it is debatable as to when the 'Then' should be. I have normally taken it to be the BR steam era, but there are cases where a location has kept changing over the years. Just as one example of this I have selected a local location for me to show the changes over the past 40 years. Starting here, a very dirty Gresley 'A3' No 60048 *Doncaster* heads the 12.30pm Leeds Central-King's Cross service past Copley Hill shed, with the carriage sheds in the background. In 1959 Copley Hill had an allocation of 33 locomotives. *Author*

Then: 29 April 1967

The shed was originally coded 37B and became 56C when the Leeds area was transferred to North Eastern Region control in 1956. It eventually closed in 1964 and the site was cleared. The carriage sidings, however, remained. The up 'Yorkshire Pullman' is pictured passing, headed by Brush Type 4 (later Class 47) No D1548 (later No 47433). *Author*

Then: 24 July 1980
By 1980 the carriage sheds had closed and a large industrial unit had been built on the site. Class 47 No 47401 is seen at the head of the 10.45 Leeds-King's Cross. The sidings have also disappeared. *Author*

Now: 5 February 1997
The site now shows the evidence of electrification. A DVT passes silently by at the head of the 12.05 Leeds-King's Cross train with a Class 91 bringing up the rear as usual. Photographically, as in so many other places, this once fine location has been ruined, not only by the paraphernalia associated with electrification, but also by, in this instance, a high aluminium fence. *Author*

Leeds Central

Then: 2 October 1962

The station opened on 18 September 1848 and was used by both the GNR and the L&YR. For a short period in the late 1840s the station was also used by the LNWR and by the Leeds & Thirsk Railway. Over the years the station was host to many famous named trains, such as the 'Yorkshire Pullman', the 'Queen of Scots Pullman', the 'West Riding Limited' and the 'White Rose' to name but a few. Unfortunately, the station did not match the glamour of the express trains that served it and certainly in its last 25 years, when I knew it well, it was a depressing and dirty place. The gradient from the platform end was 1 in 100 which often resulted in some spectacular departures when the rails were slippery. On a fine October's day 'J50' 0-6-0 No 68984 prepares to haul the empty stock off an express to Copley Hill carriage sidings for servicing. This was a service performed for many years by this locomotive alongside its sister No 68988. *Author*

Now: 5 February 1997

The station finally closed on 29 April 1967 when all surviving services were transferred to Leeds City. The site was completely cleared and acquired by the Post Office, which built these very ugly but no doubt functional buildings. It was difficult to know exactly where to stand, but I must be very near to the original spot with this picture taken from the back of the Jolly Giant toy store. *Author*

Stanningley East

Then: 5 July 1967
This location was about half-way between Leeds and Bradford on the direct route between the two cities. Services started on 1 August 1854. This illustration shows a down train from King's Cross to Bradford passing the East signalbox headed by a Type 2 (later Class 25)

No D5177 and a Fairburn 2-6-4T No 42689. This was about 10 weeks before steam operation finished in the area and these trains were being used to train drivers on diesel locomotives. *Author*

Now: 5 August 1996
Stanningley lost its station on 30 December 1967 in connection with the construction of the new parkway station at New Pudsey. Goods traffic, however, continued until 1 October 1979. Today the railway here is simply represented by the Leeds-Bradford route; there are few remains of the old goods yards. Class 158 No 158766 rushes past at 15.32 heading for Leeds. *Author*

Laisterdyke

Then: 12 March 1967
The original GNR route through Laisterdyke opened on 1 August 1854 and over the years the location developed into an important junction for the GNR, with lines heading towards Wakefield and Shipley as well as the Bradford avoiding line to link up with the L&YR at Bowling Junction. Fairburn 2-6-4T No 42073 heads eastbound with the 10.25am Bradford-King's Cross service. By the date of this photograph, Laisterdyke station had closed, losing its passenger services on 2 July 1966. *Author*

Quarry Gap Junction, Laisterdyke

Then: 30 October 1966
Fairburn 2-6-4T No 42116 of Low Moor, where it had been allocated virtually from new, heads the Bradford portion of an up King's Cross service over the route from Laisterdyke through Ardsley to Wakefield Westgate, where the train would combine with a section from Leeds. The line opened to passengers in two stages: from Laisterdyke to Gildersome on 20 August 1856 and thence to Ardsley on 10 October 1857. The line at the bottom right-hand side is the remains of the route to Shipley, which opened in 1874 to freight and the following year to passenger services. *Author*

Now: 5 August 1996
The Laisterdyke-Ardsley line lost its passenger services on 4 July 1966, and freight traffic was progressively withdrawn with the exception of the short stretch from Laisterdyke to Dudley Hill. This finally closed on 6 August 1979 simultaneously with the final stub of the closed line to Shipley that had been retained to serve a factory. Part of the land has been used subsequently for industrial development, but much is still derelict. The large mill in the left background still continues in business. *Author*

Now: 12 August 1996
All routes bar the Bradford-Leeds line have now closed, as have the numerous goods yards that once dominated the area. Apart from the main line, all that remains of the once busy location is a single siding, which receives little or no traffic. No locomotive-hauled trains are diagrammed these days, so the appearance of Class 56 No 56021 in Loadhaul livery was a rare event as it hauled an engineers' train back to Healey Mills Yard. *Author*

Bradford Hammerton Street Shed

Then: 8 January 1958
This depot, which was originally coded 37C and then 56C when transferred to North Eastern Region control, served the ex-GNR lines in and around Bradford. In its latter days it had an allocation of mainly ex-GNR 'J6s', 'N1s', 'C12s' and ex-LNER 'J39s', 'J50s' and 'B1s'. Class J39 No 64886 is shown by the coaling stage three days before all steam operations were transferred away to the ex-L&YR shed at Low Moor and Hammerton Street was dedicated to looking after the area's DMU allocation (which had first arrived in 1954). *Author*

Now: 28 August 1996
The DMU depot closed in the early 1980s when the servicing of the remaining units was transferred to Leeds Neville Hill. The buildings were left standing, however, and for a period were used to store stock acquired in connection with the proposed West Yorkshire Transport Museum project. This requirement ceased and the buildings have been subsequently demolished and, as can be seen in this illustration, the site is currently derelict. *Author*

St Dunstans (Bradford)

Then: 12 March 1967

This station was situated about half a mile from Bradford Exchange on the 1 in 50 gradient and immediately after Mill Lane Junction, where the GN lines from Laisterdyke met the ex-L&YR lines from Halifax. St Dunstans was the point where the Queensbury lines diverged from the main line towards Leeds. There was also the third side of the triangle — although lacking platforms — that gave access to Queensbury from Leeds direct through a short tunnel. Fairburn 2-6-4T No 42073 (which is now preserved on the Lakeside & Haverthwaite Railway) climbs past the station site, with the Bradford portion of a

Leeds-King's Cross train. Services to this station started in 1878, although it was closed on 15 September 1952, some three years before passenger services were withdrawn from the Queensbury line. To the left of the signalbox were carriage sidings, and the coal yards, located beyond the L&YR line, were still in use at this date. The line entered a deep cutting beyond this point as it ascended towards Laisterdyke, which in winter months frequently caused difficulties for trains through the combination of the 1 in 50 gradient and sharp curves. *Author*

Now: 4 August 1996

Locomotive-hauled trains are now extremely rare past this location, with only the very occasional special and permanent way train. Here track re-laying was being carried out on the L&YR route towards Bowling Junction. To get one Class 37 was quite an achievement, but to get another in the same picture heading down the bank towards Bradford was really stretching the odds. No 37516 in Loadhaul livery, but without the logo, climbs up the gradient *en route* to Healey Mills Yard, whilst No 37711 moves towards the Interchange to run round and take the second train back to the same location. *Author*

Bradford Exchange (south)

Then: 21 March 1967

When the GNR first reached Bradford in August 1854 it served its own terminus — Adolphus Street. Proposals for a joint L&YR/GNR station were soon developed and the new Exchange station opened in January 1867, thus consigning the original terminus to a 105-year life as a goods depot. Exchange was a 10-platform terminus station situated at the bottom of a 1 in 50 gradient ascent to Mill Lane Junction and beyond. The GNR had the eastern half of the station and the L&YR the western five platforms and in the age of steam it was a fascinating place, where the branch trains from the GNR lines were fly shunted back into the platforms once their locomotives had been released by use of the gradient. Originally the station was approached through a double-track tunnel, but this caused congestion and authority was received in July 1873 to open out the tunnel and install extra tracks. The Bradford portion of an express from King's Cross is shown arriving at the terminus headed by Class 5 No 44807. *Author*

Bradford Exchange

Then: 27 August 1967

This photograph was taken inside the impressive station about one month before the final end of main line steam operation in the area. Dating from 1867, Exchange was jointly used by the L&Y and GN railways. A work-stained Fairburn 2-6-4T No 42141 of Low Moor prepares to leave with a King's Cross train, whilst on the left is one of the Calder Valley DMU sets (later Class 110). *Author*

Shipley

Then: 7 July 1964

Although this location is more normally associated with the Midland Railway, the GNR opened a passenger station in the town at the end of its branch from Laisterdyke on 15 April 1875. A connection with the MR was also provided. As the Midland station was much nearer to the town, GNR services did not prosper and were withdrawn on 31 January 1931. The line to Shipley GN branched off at Laisterdyke Quarry Gap and ran via Idle, descending to Shipley on a 1 in 61 gradient, over which there were a number of runaways. Three months before the through services to Laisterdyke finished, immaculate Low Moor-allocated 'Jubilee' No 45694 *Bellerophon* leaves Shipley Junction past one of the then few remaining ex-GNR somersault signals in the area. At the time the Low Moor 'Jubilees' often worked this evening train as they had very little work during the week since nearly all local services were DMU operated, but they did haul summer Saturday extras to the coastal resorts. *Author*

Now: 5 August 1996

The new Bradford Exchange (later retitled Interchange) was built a few hundred yards up the gradient from the original station to alleviate problems caused by a road overbridge and in connection with the building of the new bus station. The new station opened on 15 January 1973 when two platforms were inaugurated; a further two platforms followed later. One of the West Yorkshire PTE red-liveried Class 155s, No 155347, is seen arriving at 15.58 from Leeds. The high retaining wall on the left shows how the line was opened out after the removal of the tunnel. Bradford Interchange currently has no locomotive-hauled trains, save for the occasional special or departmental working. *Author*

Now: 5 August 1996

After a life of more than a century, Bradford Exchange closed on 14 January 1973 to be replaced by a new station about 200yd up the gradient towards Mill Lane Junction. After a half life, when the bulk of the overall roof was removed, the station was finally demolished in the early 1980s. It was very difficult to know exactly where to stand for this picture, because there is absolutely nothing to guide you. The area is now a car park and new law courts have also been built on the site. The old Great Northern Hotel to the left of the picture is still in use. *Author*

Now: 5 October 1996

The section of line between Idle and Cutlers Junction Laisterdyke was closed completely on 31 October 1964. The section between Shipley and Idle was to follow on 5 October 1968. The area has now been landscaped and some industrial units built on the site. The original GNR station buildings, however, still survive. The electrified line between Bradford and Skipton is behind the trees on the right-hand side. *Author*

Queensbury

Then: 14 May 1955

The town of Queensbury is situated 1,150ft on top of the Pennines, about half-way between Bradford and Halifax, and can be a very inhospitable place as far as the weather is concerned in the winter. The station opened in 1879, but, unfortunately, it was 400ft lower than the town. Consideration was given to building an inclined tramway to link the two in both 1878 and 1887, but nothing happened. The possibility of a two-mile branch with a gradient of 1 in 30 and curves of 10 chains was also discussed, but the GNR settled for a new road, one mile long. Services to Thornton did not start until 14 April 1879 and to Halifax on 15 December 1879. The entrance to the 2,501yd-long Queensbury Tunnel was just off the platform on the Halifax line. Along with Ambergate of all pre-Grouping stations, Queensbury had one great claim to fame — it had platforms on all three sides of the triangle. An unidentified Class N1 0-6-2T is shown on the 4.46pm Bradford-Halifax train, one week before passenger services ceased over the Bradford-Queensbury-Halifax/Keighley lines. *J. F. Oxley*

Wilsden

Then: Early 1950s

This remote station was one of the intermediate stations on the Queensbury-Keighley route. Passenger services started on 7 April 1884. This undated photograph, which was probably taken shortly before services ended, shows Bradford Hammerton Street (37C)-allocated Class N1 0-6-2T No 69434 working a train from Keighley to either Bradford or Halifax. These sturdy ex-GNR locomotives dating from 1907 were the backbone of the motive power for passenger work over the lines for many years. *Ian Allan Library*

Now: 5 August 1996
Passenger services over the route were withdrawn on 23 May 1955 and the section from Queensbury to Holmfield (on the Halifax line) was closed completely on 28 May 1956. Freight services over the Bradford-Keighley section were gradually curtailed, with the line through Queensbury to Thornton succumbing on 28 June 1965. As can be seen, there is now nothing to remind you that this was the site where the platforms had once stood. The land, which was at the head of a valley, had been originally partially filled in to allow for the construction of the station; this process has continued since demolition. *Author*

Now: 13 August 1996
Passenger services over the route were withdrawn on 23 May 1955 and freight traffic between Thornton and Cullingworth ceased on 11 November 1963. A new house has now been built on the site and the cutting filled in. Behind the trees in the background of this picture one can still find the road bridge, which has been filled in. *Author*

Holmfield

Then: 29 June 1960
This was the junction where the Halifax High Level line to St Pauls met the Halifax-Queensbury line and was jointly controlled by the GN and L&Y railways through the Halifax & Ovenden Joint. Passenger services on the main line started in 1879 and the High Level route opened for all traffic on 5 September 1890. The platforms for the branch were just to the left of the picture. Passenger services to St Pauls were shortlived and were withdrawn on 31 December 1916. Those on the through route were to survive until 23 May 1955. All traffic north of Holmfield ceased on 26 May 1956. Services beyond Halifax North Bridge to Holmfield and to St Pauls were withdrawn on 27 June 1960 and two days later Newton Heath Class 5, No 45339, an unusual locomotive for the line, collected the last wagons. I travelled on the footplate of this train as it was my local line. I forget the number of unfitted wagons we had, but it was a long train, and we set off down the 1 in 50 gradient towards Halifax. It was intended that I would alight at North Bridge station, but the wagons thought differently. In a scene which was reminiscent of the antics of the trucks in 'Thomas the Tank Engine', we passed non-stop with all wheels locked and eventually stopped about 400yd further on. *Author*

Now: 5 August 1996
The whole station area and the goods yard, which used to be behind where I took this photograph, have been developed into an industrial estate. The Smith Bulmer mill in the background still exists, but not for its original purpose. *Author*

Pellon

Then: 24 May 1959

This station was situated on the Halifax High Level line, which was jointly operated by the Great Northern and Lancashire & Yorkshire railways. The line was opened on 27 June 1890 for freight and to passengers on 5 September the same year, although the latter lasted only until 31 December 1916. Freight continued, however, until 27 June 1960. By the date of this photograph, freight traffic had dwindled to almost nothing. Sowerby Bridge 'WD' 2-8-0 No 90122 is shown ready to leave for Holmfield with the 5.15pm train. The island platform was still *in situ*, despite having been out of use for more than 40 years. The stations of Halifax St Pauls and Halifax Town were only about one mile apart, but there was a difference in height of 325ft. *Author*

Now: 5 August 1996

The site has been developed into an industrial area. The viaduct at the bottom of the incline from Pellon which crossed the Wheatley Valley about one mile from Pellon still stands. *Author*

Hull Cannon Street

Then: 1932

The Hull & Barnsley's terminus in Hull was originally designed as a carriage shed as the company intended to extend its line nearer to the city centre. When this did not materialise, the shed was adopted as the terminus and it was extended during the early 1890s. Passenger services over the line commenced on 27 July 1885. Initially there were 13 departures per day from Cannon Street during the week. When the H&BR had been proposed, it had been the plan that a connection between it and the NER would be constructed at Spring Bank; when this was finally opened, in 1924, it enabled the ex-H&BR services to be transferred to Paragon and Cannon Street was closed to passenger services from 14 July 1924.
Ian Allan Library (19352)

Hull & Barnsley Railway

Few parts of the country were dominated by a single railway company as the northeast of England. From the Humber Estuary to north of the River Tyne, one company — the North Eastern Railway — exercised almost total control. It was in an effort to break this near monopoly that the Hull & Barnsley Railway was promoted. It was planned as a route that would offer an alternative — and competitive line — between the Yorkshire coalfield and the port of Hull, through which the coal could be exported.

Originally incorporated as the Hull, Barnsley & West Riding Junction Railway & Dock Co in 1880 — the name was simplified to Hull & Barnsley Railway in 1905 — the H&BR's line was effectively one route heading west from Hull to Wrangbrook Junction, where it split into three. One route headed west towards Cudworth and Barnsley, a second headed southwestwards towards Wath and a third ran south to Conisbrough. The company was also authorised to extend further into the West Riding, but nothing came of these proposals.

The main line opened between Hull and Cudworth on 20 July 1885 for freight traffic and 27 July the same year for passenger services. At the Cudworth end, the line was extended to Stairfoot (three miles) and Monk Bretton (half a mile) at the same time; these sections carried freight only. The line from Wrangbrook Junction to Denaby & Conisbrough opened for freight on 1 September 1894 and to passenger trains on the following 1 December. The third route from Wrangbrook Junction — that to Wath — opened to freight on 31 March 1902 and to passengers on the following 23 August.

In addition to its own lines, the H&B had a share with the GCR in the line from Aire Junction to Warmsworth, which opened for freight

Now: 22 June 1996
Cannon Street continued as a freight depot until 3 June 1868. The 'Now' photograph shows that virtually nothing survives to indicate that there was once a railway terminus on the site. The former railway land has now been occupied by a company called Parmac Engineering Services. *Author*

traffic on 1 May 1916, and thence to Braithwell (which opened the following 4 December). From Braithwell, the line continued south towards Shireoaks; this route was jointly controlled by the GCR, the H&BR and the MR and opened for freight on 1 October 1909.

Despite the potential traffic, the H&BR was an impecunious railway — indeed the section from Wrangbrook Junction to Denaby & Conisbrough had already lost its passenger services (on 2 February 1903) — and at various times amalgamation with either the Midland or Great Central railways was proposed. In the event, it was to be the NER that took the line over from 1 April 1922. The takeover allowed for the process of rationalisation to begin. The first stage was the construction of the long-proposed link in Hull, which allowed the H&BR's Cannon Street station to be closed with services transferred to Paragon.

Passenger services over Wath-Wrangbrook Junction section were withdrawn on 6 April 1929. These were followed on 1 January 1932 by the withdrawal of passenger services between South Howden and Cudworth, leaving the section from South Howden to Hull to continue until 1 August 1955.

Following the withdrawal of passenger services, the line continued to see considerable freight traffic, but post-Nationalisation the route was further rationalised. Following the withdrawal of passenger services over the eastern section, the route between Wrangbrook Junction and Little Weighton was closed completely on 6 April 1959; the section from Little Weighton to Hull followed on 6 July 1964. The section from Wrangbrook Junction to Moorhouse & South Elmsall followed on 30 September 1963 (the section south from Moorhouse to Wath having closed on 31 May 1954). This was followed on 7 August 1967 by the closure of the sections from Wrangbrook Junction to Cudworth and to Denaby & Conisbrough. This left the only operational section of the erstwhile H&B line as the route running to the docks to the east of Hull. It was, however, not quite the end of the story, because in 1972 the section between Hensall Junction and Drax reopened for merry-go-round trains serving the coal-fired power station.

Willerby & Kirk Ella

Then: 13 November 1954
Situated about six miles from the terminus at Cannon Street and about half-way between the two villages that provided it with its name, the station at Willerby & Kirk Ella was opened for passenger services on 27 July 1885. Prior to 1941 Sentinel railcars worked the passenger service, but then the Class G5 0-4-4Ts took over, running a push/pull service. One of the class, No 67337, is seen at the station on the Saturdays Only 11.45am Hull Paragon-South Howden working. Passenger services over the full Hull-Cudworth route had been withdrawn back in 1932, leaving only a Hull-South Howden service, which was to survive until the mid-1950s. *J. F. Oxley*

Now: 22 June 1996
The Hull-South Howden services were withdrawn from 1 August 1955, the last of operation being 30 July 1955 when No 67337 hauled the final train. Through freight services were withdrawn in November 1958 and the section between Springfield Junction, Hull, and Little Weighton closed completely on 6 July 1964. It was rather difficult to work out exactly where to stand to be in the same spot as the 'Then' picture, as the embankment that used to exist had been flattened and these houses built on the site. About 300yd away at the end of a car park, the trackbed could be seen. *Author*

Little Weighton

Then: Autumn 1963
By the date of this photograph, rationalisation had already reduced the status of Little Weighton as an intermediate point on the H&BR. Passenger services over the line between Hull and South Howden had succumbed on 1 August 1955 and in November 1958 through mineral trains over the line had been withdrawn. Complete closure of the section of the line from Little Weighton to Wrangbrook Junction came on 6 April 1959. The section eastbound, however, was retained for freight for a further five years. *R. Prattey*

Now: 14 December 1996
The final closure of the line east from Little Weighton to Hull came on 6 July 1964. Nearly 33 years after services finished, the station appears to be in the process of renovation and will no doubt make a very fine private property. Little Weighton was at the summit of the climb on to the Wolds. *Author*

South Cave

Then: September 1957
Opened in 1885, South Cave was to the west of Little Weighton. 'Austerity' 2-8-0 No 90523, with an eastbound coal train, climbs the seven-mile 1 in 150 gradient to the summit of the line at the east end of the one-mile 356yd-long Drewton Tunnel. Compared with the ex-NER line out of Hull, which ran along the side of the Humber Estuary, the H&BR had a steep climb on an inland route to the top of the Yorkshire Wolds. By the date of this photograph, South Cave had already lost its passenger services (on 1 August 1955). *A. M. Ross*

Drax (Abbey)

Then: Undated
This undated photograph shows the station after the withdrawal of passenger services (which occurred on the section west of South Howden on 1 January 1932) and probably around the time of complete closure in April 1959. The station, known as 'Drax' to the H&BR, became Drax Abbey to differentiate it from the NER station, although this didn't occur until after Nationalisation when it was served only by freight trains. *A. P. Hincliffe*

Carlton Towers

Then: May 1957
Passenger services over the H&BR commenced in 1885, but were withdrawn over the section west from South Howden to Cudworth on 1 January 1932. The fact that this shows a passenger train suggests that it is probably an enthusiasts' special. The station is on the right.
Ian Allan Library (K3401)

Now: 14 December 1996
Through mineral workings over the route ceased on 29 November 1959 and the section west from Little Weighton to Wrangbrook Junction closed completely in April 1959. As can be seen, the station and yard still existed. Now privately owned, a business is operated from the yard. *Author*

Now: 14 December 1996
The house/station is now privately owned, but the trackbed is owned by somebody else (who occupies a house nearer to where the level crossing used to be, about 400yd from where I am standing). The trackbed and immediate area is now full of various old tractors, wagons, cars, etc, which seem to be virtually abandoned. *Author*

Now: 14 December 1996
Through mineral trains over the route were withdrawn in November 1958 and the section between Little Weighton and Wrangbrook Junction closed completely the following April. However, the four-mile section between Hensall Junction and Drax was reopened in 1972 for the MGR traffic to Drax power station. This section of track is now extremely busy with coal trains. It is the only part of the H&BR route outside Hull that is still active. The station is now privately owned and has been made into a fine property. *Author*

Sutton Bridge

Then: Undated
This view shows Sutton Bridge station looking towards Spalding. The first station at Sutton Bridge opened on 3 July 1862 and the station illustrated here was the third station to serve the town, being completed in 1897. Sutton Bridge was the junction for the M&GN trains heading west to Spalding and south to Peterborough. The swing bridge, which carried the railway and what is now the A17 road across the River Nene, is located about 200yd behind the photographer. *Ian Allan Library (23404)*

Now: 14 November 1996
As from 2 March 1959 the sections of the ex-M&GN eastwards towards South Lynn and southwards to Peterborough were closed completely. This left Sutton Bridge as the terminus of a freight-only route from Spalding. This was to survive until 5 April 1965 when the section was to close completely. The station site is now occupied by a company called Metalair Filliat, which produces road tankers. The swing bridge is still in use, although the former railway side now carries the westbound road traffic. *Author*

South Lynn

Then: 4 October 1958
Looking east at South Lynn, the junction is clearly shown. The lines to the left headed towards King's Lynn, whilst those straight on formed the main line to Melton Constable and Yarmouth. The station first opened on 1 January 1886. Here one of the many Ivatt Class 4MT 2-6-0s allocated to the line, No 43111, leaves with the 1.16pm train from Peterborough to Yarmouth Beach. *F. Church*

Midland & Great Northern Joint Railway

The Midland & Great Northern Joint Railway was established on 1 July 1893, although its roots were much earlier, and as its name implies was jointly controlled by the Midland and Great Northern Railways. The railway comprised just over 130 route miles, the vast majority of which was single track. The network stretched from Little Bytham (where an end-on junction was made with the Midland) and Peterborough in the west through to Norwich, Cromer and Great Yarmouth in the east. The line's major junction was at Melton Constable, where the company's workshops were established. In addition to its own line, the M&GNJR also had a share, with the GER, in the two sections of the Norfolk & Suffolk Joint lines, from North Walsham to Cromer and from Yarmouth to Lowestoft.

The first part of the future M&GN to open was the Spalding-Holbeach section of the Norwich & Spalding Railway on 9 August 1858 for freight and 15 November 1858 for passenger traffic. This was extended to Sutton Bridge on 1 July 1862. The opening of the Lynn & Sutton Bridge Railway for freight traffic followed in November 1864. The line between Spalding and Bourne opened on 1 August 1866 and on the same day the Peterborough, Wisbech & Sutton Bridge line opened to passenger traffic (it had opened to freight on 1 June 1866). The final section in the west, the link between Bourne and Saxby (with an end-on junction at Little Bytham) opened on 5 June 1893 to freight and to passengers on 1 May 1894.

In the east, the first section to be opened was that between Great Yarmouth and Ormesby of the Great Yarmouth & Stalham Light Railway (later Yarmouth & North Norfolk), which opened on 7 August 1877. This was extended to Hemsby on 16 May 1878. Following problems in building the bridge at Potter Heigham, the next section, to Catfield, opened on 17 January 1880 and thence to Stalham itself on 3 July 1880. By this date the company had been authorised to extend the line to North Walsham; this opened on 13 June 1881. Almost contemporary with these developments, the Lynn & Fakenham Railway was under construction. The first section, from Lynn to Massingham, opened on 16 August 1879 and the line was completed through to Fakenham on 6 August 1880. The line was extended, via Melton Constable, to Guestwick on 19 January 1882 and then to Lenwade on 1 July 1882. It was at this time that the works at Melton Contable were established. In Great Yarmouth, the Yarmouth Union line, which provided a link between the town's three stations, was opened on 15 May 1882. Finally in 1882, the line between Lenwade and Norwich was opened on 2 December. In early 1883 the Y&NN and L&F merged to form the Eastern & Midlands Railway.

The next section to be completed was that between Melton Constable and North Walsham, which was opened on 5 April 1883. This was followed with the opening of the Melton Constable-Holt section on 1 October 1884 and thence to Cromer on 16 June 1887. This was the last extension to the eastern section prior to the creation of the M&GNJR in 1893.

The Norfolk & Suffolk line from North Walsham to Mundesley opened to freight traffic on 20 June 1898 and to passenger services on 1 July the same year. On 13 July 1903 the M&GNJR's link to the Lowestoft line opened to Gorleston North; at the same time the N&S line between Lowestoft and Great Yarmouth was also opened. This was followed in 1906 by the completion of the Cromer-Mundesley line. These developments effectively completed the M&GNJR empire.

At the Grouping in 1923 the shares in the M&GNJR were divided between the LMS and the LNER and this arrangement persisted until 1 October 1936, when the LNER took over sole operation of the line. In 1948 control passed to the Eastern Region of the newly formed British Railways. Inevitably, given the essentially rural area through which much of the M&GN operated, the financial pressures that affected the railway industry during the 1950s had a severe impact on the M&GN section, and the post-Nationalisation period witnessed an inexorable decline in the facilities provided.

The first section to lose its passenger services was that between Cromer and Mundesley, which succumbed on 7 April 1953 at which time this section closed completely. This closure was followed on 2 March 1959 by the closure of the bulk of the M&GN network. On this date the passenger services were withdrawn from the route from Saxby to Great Yarmouth and from Peterborough to Sutton Bridge. The majority of the lines also closed to freight traffic at the same time. The line from Norwich to Melton Constable also lost its passenger services on 2 March 1959, but remained open for freight traffic. This closure was followed on 6 April 1964 by the withdrawal of passenger services between Melton Constable and Sheringham. With the opening of a new curve at Themelthorpe in 1964, providing access to the ex-GER line to Wroxham, the section from Themelthorpe to Sheringham was closed completely in 1964 (it has subsequently been reinstated by preservationists between Sheringham and Holt). Passenger services were withdrawn between North Walsham and Mundesley on 5 October 1964, and passenger services over the N&S line between Lowestoft and Great Yarmouth ceased on 4 May 1970. The last significant stretch of the M&GN retained for freight operation — that to Norwich — was gradually cut back, to Drayton on 3 February 1969, to Lenwade, and then withdrawn completely on 15 June 1983.

Today the only sections of the M&GN to survive are those from Sheringham to Holt, which is now the preserved North Norfolk Railway, and the branch between Sheringham and Cromer, which continues to see regular passenger services to Norwich.

Now: 14 November 1996
Passenger services through South Lynn were withdrawn from 2 March 1959 and from the same day the section west to Sutton Bridge was closed completely. The link to King's Lynn reamined open for freight as did the ex-main line eastwards to East Rudham; the latter closed completely on 6 May 1968. The link to King's Lynn survived until the early 1990s, but as can be seen here, there is evidence of recent track lifting. The bulk of the site has become a caravan park. *Author*

Melton West Junction

Then: 30 August 1958
This fine photograph shows Ivatt Class 4MT 2-6-0 No 43158 approaching Melton Constable station with the 9.33am summer Saturdays Only service from Derby to Yarmouth Beach. This was to be the last year that through services operated. Another Ivatt 2-6-0 can be seen on the Cromer line. *G. R. Mortimer*

Now: 14 November 1996
The line to South Lynn was to close completely on 2 March 1959. However, the line to Cromer was to survive longer. Freight services to Norwich City ran via Cromer, Sheringham and Melton Constable until the construction of a new link at Themelthorpe enabled services to be diverted in September 1960. Melton West box was closed on 1 January 1961 and, finally, passenger services between Sheringham and Melton Constable were withdrawn on 6 April 1964. The changes here are dramatic as there is nothing to show that a railway ever existed here. The tower on the left skyline is the only marker point between the two pictures. The bus shelter a few yards from this point had a fine painting of an M&GN 4-4-2T in it. *Author*

Sheringham

Then: 31 August 1960
The railway station here was first opened on 16 June 1887, and Sheringham became an important destination, especially in the holiday season. In latter days, such prestigious trains as the 'Broadsman' and the 'Norfolkman', occasionally hauled by 'Britannias', called here. By the date of this photograph, the bulk of the passenger services over the ex-M&GN system had been withdrawn, leaving a service from Melton Constable to Norwich via Sheringham and Cromer. Here a Metro-Cammell DMU (later Class 101) is seen ready to return to Norwich. The goods yard is over to the right of the picture. *A. Moore*

Melton Constable

Then: 8 August 1958
This was the centre of the M&GNR, where the railway's workshops and main locomotive shed were based. The station was first opened on 19 January 1882 and grew with the gradual expansion of the M&GN system. Although less well known than other railway towns, the M&GN was the major local employer. This illustration shows one of the large group of 34 Ivatt Class 4MT 2-6-0s that were allocated to the ex-M&GN from new, and which were based at South Lynn, Melton Constable and Yarmouth Beach. The works closed on 1 January 1937 (locomotive section) but remained open for wagons and coaching stock thereafter, and the shed in February 1959 after having been rebuilt as late as 1951. No 43110 is on the platform avoiding line with a down goods for Great Yarmouth, whilst a DMU for Sheringham stands in the platform. *F. Church*

Now: 14 November 1996
Passenger services over the lines west to South Lynn, east to Yarmouth and south to Norwich City were all withdrawn on 2 March 1959 (the last services having operated on 28 February 1959). The sections west to East Rudham and east to North Walsham were closed completely at the same time. This left freight operations to Norwich City from the north and the remaining passenger link via Holt to Sheringham. The former were withdrawn on 12 September 1960 with the opening of the Themelthorpe link. Finally, the passenger service between Melton Constable and Sheringham was withdrawn on 28 December 1964. The station area is now an industrial estate and, unfortunately, there were no points of direct comparison between the two periods. I am, however, certain that I was standing in the right location. The buildings from the railway works still stand and are in industrial use. *Author*

Now: 15 November 1996
The passenger service between Sheringham and Melton Constable was withdrawn on 28 December 1964 at which time the section west of Melton Constable was closed completely. This was not, however, the end of the story as the station became the base of the nascent North Norfolk Railway. BR services to this station were withdrawn on 2 February 1967 with the opening of a new station to the east of the level crossing. As the station was full of rolling stock, a directly comparable view would have shown little of the current scene. As a result I have taken the 'Now' picture from the road bridge. The current Railtrack station is now on the other side of the road beyond the stock in the station. The well-restored NNR station has three platforms, but most of the old yard is now the inevitable car park. No services were running when I visited on this occasion, although the preserved Class B12 4-6-0 was running light engine on driver-training duties. My thanks are due to the railway's staff, as they were extremely helpful and friendly. The Class 08 diesel shunter visible is ex-BR No 08767. *Author*

Cromer Beach

Then: 26 June 1929
The terminus station at Cromer Beach opened on 16 June 1887. This photograph, taken in the period before the LNER took over operation of the railway, shows one of the M&GN 4-4-2Ts No 20, of a type that was to be classified C17 under the LNER. No 20 was one of three of the type built between 1904 and 1910; it was withdrawn in 1942. *H. C. Casserley*

Then: 24 August 1979
This intermediate photograph, taken after Cromer Beach lost its freight facilities (on 31 January 1969), shows that the immediate station area had not altered much over 50 years, although the goods yard had been ripped up. A Class 105 Cravens-built unit is ready to leave on the 15.26 service to Norwich. *Author*

Now: 15 November 1996
The station is still in use and here Class 153 No 153335 is pictured ready to depart on the 08.45 service from Sheringham to Norwich. Facilities are now reduced to a minimum. The yard to the left has now been developed into a Safeway supermarket. The signalbox at the end of the platform is still in use. *Author*

Corpusty & Saxthorpe

Then: 8 August 1958
This was the first station to the east of Melton Constable on the line towards Yarmouth. The station opened on 5 April 1883. Ex-Great Eastern Class J15 0-6-0 No 65551 heads a freight towards Melton Constable. *F. Church*

Now: 14 November 1996
Passenger services over the bulk of the ex-M&GN were withdrawn on 2 March 1959 and on the same day the section between Melton Constable and North Walsham Town was closed completely. As can be seen, there have been extensive earthworks undertaken since closure and the site has been levelled. The old station building has remained intact and has been used as a sports centre. *Author*

North Walsham Town

Then: 17 May 1948
The Great Eastern and M&GN stations in North Walsham were only about 200yd apart, on opposite sides of the main road through the town. The latter was opened on 13 June 1881. One of the handsome ex-GER Class D16/3 4-4-0s, No 2592, calls at the station with the 10.35am Peterborough North-Yarmouth Beach service. *W. A. Camwell*

Now: 15 November 1996
Passenger services between Melton Constable and Yarmouth Beach via North Walsham Town were withdrawn from 2 March 1959 and at the same time the sections west from North Walsham to Melton Constable and east from North Walsham to Yarmouth closed completely. This left North Walsham Town, served by a spur off the ex-GER route (built in 1958), to survive as a freight destination until complete closure on 1 January 1966. Part of the station site has now been occupied by Horners Auctioneers. I arrived on the day of an auction, so I stayed and watched the proceedings for a while — I was amazed at what appeared to me to be junk, but which was obviously selling very well — before asking some locals to confirm that I was at the correct location. *Author*

North British Railway

Whilst the North British Railway was the largest of the Scottish-based railway companies, it had played a game of corporate cat and mouse with the North Eastern Railway in Northumberland, which had resulted in a small network of lines south of the border.

These routes were the line linking Hexham with Riccarton Junction on the main line from Carlisle to Edinburgh (the Border Counties line), the route from Reedsmouth to Morpeth and the branch from Scotsgap Junction to Rothbury.

The first section of line to be opened was the five-mile stretch from Hexham to Chollerton which commenced operation on 5 April 1858. This was followed on 1 December 1859 by the stretch from Chollerton to Reedsmouth. The line was completed through to Riccarton Junction on 2 June 1862 for freight traffic and on the following 1 July for passenger services. This was followed on 23 July 1862 by the opening of the line between Scotsgap and Morpeth; the link between Scotsgap and Reedsmouth was opened on 1 May 1865. From Scotsgap Junction, the branch to Rothbury was opened on 1 November 1870, thereby completing the NBR network in Northumberland.

All the routes passed intact firstly to the LNER and then to BR. However, the rationalisation of the 1950s was to bring closure. First to succumb were the passenger services between Morpeth and Reedsmouth and over the Rothbury branch, both of which were withdrawn on 15 September 1952. Passenger services over the Border Counties line from Hexham to Riccarton Junction followed on 15 October 1956. These closures were followed by the withdrawal of all freight over the Border Counties line, with the exception of the section from Bellingham to Reedsmouth Junction, on 1 September 1958. On 11 September 1963 freight services were withdrawn on the Bellingham-Woodburn and Rothbury-Scotsgap Junction sections. Finally, on 3 October 1966, freight services were withdrawn from the Woodburn-Morpeth route, bringing to an end the presence of former NBR lines in Northumberland.

In addition to the Northumberland lines, the NBR also had a presence in the west, with the Border Union main line reaching Carlisle and with the branches to Port Carlisle and Silloth, but these are outside the scope of this volume.

Humshaugh

Then: 12 October 1956
This was the second station out of Hexham on the Border Counties line towards Reedsmouth Junction and Riccarton Junction. The line beyond Chollerford through Humshaugh to Reedsmouth was opened on 1 December 1859. This photograph, taken only a few days before the line closed to passenger services, shows an extremely dirty Class K1 2-6-0 No 62023 working a train from Hexham. The station gardens had obviously been well cared for in the past. *W. A. Camwell*

Now: 10 June 1996
Passenger services over the Border Counties line were withdrawn from 15 October 1956 and freight on the section between Hexham and Reedsmouth Junction followed on 1 September 1958. As with a number of the other substantial station buildings in the region, Humshaugh has now been converted into a superb house; of the ones seen during the preparation of this book, Humshaugh was one of the most impressive. *Author*

Reedsmouth Junction

Then: Undated *circa* mid-1950s
Reedsmouth was one of the those locations whose importance to the railways outweighed its actual status. This was the point where the Border Counties line, from Hexham to Riccarton Junction (which opened in stages between April 1858 and July 1862), met the line from Morpeth (which was opened from Scotsgap Junction in 1865). In this view the lines to the left head off to Riccarton Junction and those to the right towards Morpeth. The locomotive is a Class J21 0-6-0, probably No 65013 which was operating in the area before withdrawal in 1955.
Neville Stead Collection

Bellingham

Then: Undated; probably mid-1950s
Bellingham was the first station north of Reedsmouth on the Border Counties line. This section of the line was opened on 1 February 1861. This view was taken looking towards Riccarton Junction and shows a rake of Metro-Cammell DMUs. These units, later designated Class 101, were introduced only in 1956 and so the photograph is most probably of an enthusiasts' special, given that passenger services over the route were withdrawn on 15 October 1956. *Neville Stead Collection*

Woodburn

Then: Undated
The line linking Reedsmouth Junction with Scotsgap Junction opened in 1865. This view was taken from the main road overbridge looking east towards Scotsgap. It shows a freight calling at the station, headed by Class J27 0-6-0 No 65869.
Neville Stead Collection

North Eastern Railway

The largest of the constituent companies of the LNER in 1923 was the North Eastern Railway and, in historical terms, it could also lay claim, through its incorporation of the Stockton & Darlington Railway, to be the oldest part of the network, with its origins dating back to 1825.

The NER itself was formed on 31 July 1854 from a union of three earlier companies — the York, Newcastle & Berwick (incorporated on 9 July 1847), the Leeds Northern (1849) and the York & North Midland (1836). Of these companies, the YN&BR and Y&NMR were also the results of earlier mergers. The YN&BR was a union of the York & Newcastle (1846; itself a union, largely comprised of the Newcastle & Darlington Junction Railway of 1842 which opened between Newcastle and Darlington on 18 June 1844) with the Newcastle & Berwick (authorised in 1845 and opened two years later). The Y&NMR was authorised in 1836 to link York with the Leeds & Selby (which it took over in May 1844) and opened in 1839/40; the Y&NMR expanded through the take-over of the Whitby & Pickering Railway (authorised 1833; opened in 1835/36), the Hull & Selby Railway (authorised 1836; opened 1840) and East & West Yorkshire Junction Railway (linking York with Knaresborough; authorised in 1846 and opened in two stages in 1848 and 1851) in 1852. Prior to its amalgamation into the NER, the Y&NMR saw a number of further lines built. Behind many of these machinations, prior to his disgrace, was the 'Railway King' — George Hudson — but his colourful career falls outside the scope of this book.

The earliest constituent of the NER was, however, the Stockton & Darlington Railway, which was incorporated in 1821 and opened four years later, on 27 September 1825. The line was extended to Middlesbrough in December 1830 and the company continued to grow through new construction and mergers until it was itself merged into the North Eastern Railway on 13 July 1863. Amongst lines incorporated into the S&D prior to its merger with the NER was the line across Stainmore, with its dramatic viaduct at Belah.

Other early constituents of the NER included the Newcastle & Carlisle Railway (incorporated in 1829 and opened in stages between 1835 and 1838 with the Alston branch opening in 1852; merged with the NER in 1862) and the Leeds & Thirsk Railway (incorporated 1845 and opening in 1848/49 — the section through to Leeds being delayed due to the construction of Bramhope Tunnel; the line became the Leeds Northern Railway in 1851 with lines opening to Knaresborough in August 1851 and to Stockton in May 1852 before being vested in the YN&BR prior to the formation of the NER).

Serving as it did, the industrial areas of Northumberland and Durham, the NER operated an intricate network of lines that served the numerous coal mines and quarries that abounded in the region. It also served many of the most popular of the East Coast holiday resorts, such as Scarborough, Bridlington and Filey, along with the rich agricultural lands of the Vale of York. Few railways achieved such a regional domination of such a rich area as the NER and it is surprising, given the level of competition that existed in much less fertile regions for railway operation, that the NER did not face greater competition. The only serious challenge to its control came with the promotion and opening of the Hull & Barnsley Railway, but this proved to be less of a threat than it might have been and the NER had the final laugh when the H&BR merged with it in 1922, prior to the 1923 Grouping.

In the 70 years of the NER's actual existence, between 1854 and the Grouping of 1923, the railway expanded from a route mileage of some 700 to more than 1,750. It bequeathed to the LNER a significant portion of the East Coast main line, some of the finest stations in the country (such as York, Darlington, Hull Paragon and Newcastle), an electrified suburban system in and Newcastle and massive freight traffic. The period of the Grouping was, as elsewhere, to see the domination of the railways diminish as the internal combustion engine developed and there were a number of closures during the period, but the bulk of the NER was to pass to British Railways on its formation in 1948.

Over the past 50 years, the former NER empire has shrunk considerably, again mirroring events elsewhere, and many famous lines have disappeared. For the NER this decline has been even more spectacular as a result of the loss of many of the traditional heavy industries of the northeast, of which the closure of the Consett steelworks in the early 1980s and the demise of much of the remains of the coal mining industry after the strike of 1984/85 were but the latest examples. Amongst the lines to have disappeared are the Stainmore route across the Pennines, the old Leeds & Thirsk route through Ripon, the routes to Hornsea and Withernsea, all the routes that served Market Weighton, the coastal route from Scarborough to Whitby and beyond, and many others. Despite these closures, however, there is still much of the old NER network surviving; with the Nationalised railways now a thing of the past, the remaining lines, now part of Railtrack's empire, see trains from a number of Train Operating Companies, including, ironically, a company (GNER) that shares the initials of one of the old railways that helped establish the NER's prominence.

Leeds City

Then: 15 November 1960
Leeds Neville Hill-based Class A3 Pacific No 60086 *Gainsborough* has just arrived at Leeds City, as the station was then known, on the 9.55am from Newcastle to Liverpool Lime Street. The 'A3' would be exchanged on this occasion for a rebuilt 'Royal Scot' and a 'Patriot' for the journey over the Pennines. The station carried the name Leeds New until 1938, when it was amalgamated with the older Wellington station and became Leeds City. *Author*

Now: 15 April 1996
The old Leeds City station was rebuilt and the track reorganised from the early 1960s. The work, and the reduction in services consequent upon the Beeching cuts, allowed for the closure of Leeds Central and for the platforms in the former Wellington station to be used solely for parcels traffic. Today the station is probably used by as many trains as the three old stations combined. It is extremely busy and was electrified as part of the East Coast main line electrification scheme and the more recent suburban scheme covering the Skipton and Ilkley routes. Class 158 No 158771 arrives with a service from across the Pennines, whilst local West Yorkshire PTE Class 141s await departure with services for Huddersfield and the Aire Valley. *Author*

Leeds City

Then: 16 October 1963
A dramatic view of the western end of Leeds City station shows the reconstruction work already in progress. The frames of the new overall roof are in place at this end, whilst the variety of trains emphasises that operations in the station continued whilst the work progressed. *British Rail*

Now: 15 April 1996
Today the railway has been electrified and the 'new' Leeds City station approaches its 30th birthday. Although the main station retains a fairly complex network of track, the decline in parcels traffic has meant considerable rationalisation on the approaches to the former Midland station Wellington. Tracks have been replaced with that ubiquitous symbol of urban redevelopment, the car park. Much of the surrounding area has also been improved. *Author*

Wetherby

Then: Whitsun 1962
There used to be a triangle at Wetherby, connecting lines to Harrogate, Tadcaster and Leeds. In this view, empty stock trains for specials to the local racecourse wait to return over the south-to-east curve. The train on the left is for Bradford and is headed by Manningham-allocated 2–6-0 'Crab' No 42762, whilst the one on the right is for Leeds City and is headed by Neville Hill-allocated 'B16' 4-6-0 No 61429. Passenger train services were withdrawn from Wetherby on 6 January 1964, with freight services following on 4 April 1966. *J. M. Rayner*

Now: 20 April 1996
A junction, but only of footpaths, still exists at the site, but as can be seen in this picture, nature has taken over. The closure of the line between Harrogate and Leeds via Wetherby must be a cause for regret locally, as the level of road traffic has increased dramatically over the past 30 years. *Author*

Spofforth

Then: 25 September 1963
The Harrogate-Wetherby line used to cross the busy road between the same two towns at a level crossing, from where this photograph was taken. The late Lord Garnock's preserved Class K4 2-6-0 No 3442 *The Great Marquess* was being used for an inspection special of the lines in the area. The station at Spofforth opened on 10 August 1847. It is believed that the special was being run in connection with the closure of the route, which took place on 4 January 1964. *Author*

Arthington

Then: 25 April 1964
This was another triangular junction, where the line from Ilkley and Otley met the Leeds-Harrogate via Horsforth route. The first station at Arthington opened in 1865. There were four platforms at the station, two on the Harrogate-Leeds line and two on the spur from Leeds towards Otley. Headed by the last of the handsome 'B16/2' 4-6-0s, No 61435, a Railway Correspondence & Travel Society special passes the station as it heads north towards Harrogate. *M. York*

Otley

Then: 23 June 1966
The line from Arthington to Otley was opened by the North Eastern Railway on 1 February 1865. From Otley westwards to Ilkley, which opened on 1 August 1865, the line was owned by the Otley & Ilkley Joint Railway. The O&IJR was jointly owned by the North Eastern and Midland railways and thus by the LNER and LMS after 1923. The route, from Arthington to the Ilkley-Guiseley line, through Wharfedale was closed to passenger services on 22 March 1965 and to freight on 5 July the same year. By June 1966 the demolition work was well advanced at Otley station, with Stanier '8F' 2-8-0 No 48352 in attendance. *Author*

Now: 20 April 1996
Thirty years after closure, the site was being redeveloped. The only indication that there was once a railway station at this point was a small part of the platform edge at the back of the building site. *Author*

Now: 20 April 1996
The station lost its freight facilities on 25 April 1964 and passenger services on 23 March 1965. Whilst the line westwards towards Otley has closed, the line between Leeds and Harrogate remains open, although today virtually nothing remains to indicate the presence of the station except for some evidence of the up platform. The trackbed of the closed sections of the triangle remains as well. Pacer Class 144 No 144022, on the 16.28 from Leeds to York, passes the station site. *Author*

Now: 20 April 1996
Although the western extremity of the O&IJR from Ilkley to Guiseley now forms part of the electrified services to Leeds and Bradford, little evidence of the railway remains in Otley. The current picture tells its own story, with the former railway trackbed being utilised as part of a much-needed Otley bypass. *Author*

Pannal

Then: 25 September 1963
The station at Pannal, situated on the Leeds-Harrogate via Horsforth line, opened on 1 September 1848. The preserved ex-LNER 2-6-0

No 3442 is seen again, waiting in the siding with a special for an up service to pass. *Author*

Now: 20 April 1996
The station remains open and is served by a half-hourly service between Leeds and Harrogate, although the sidings and signalbox have gone. The station buildings survive, albeit converted into a restaurant. Class 144 No 144016, in West Yorkshire PTE livery, pauses in the station with the 16.05 service from Knaresborough to Leeds. Locomotive-hauled trains are now rare on the line, a great contrast to the days of the 'Queen of Scots' and 'Yorkshire Pullman' expresses headed by Eastern Pacifics. *Author*

Harrogate

Then: 1953

The original station in Harrogate was Brunswick, but this was replaced with the station on the present site in August 1862. The town used to be a busy railway centre, with routes heading to York, Ripon, Leeds, Wetherby and to Pateley Bridge. It is a spa town and was well served by Pullman services, such as the 'Queen of Scots' and the 'Yorkshire Pullman', which provided through services to King's Cross. It was from a hotel in Harrogate that the famous crime writer Agatha Christie made a mysterious (but temporary) disappearance in the 1920s. *Ian Allan Library (L&GRP 18393)*

Now: 20 April 1996

Harrogate's importance as a railway centre declined with the closure of the main line through Ripon and of the line to Leeds via Wetherby. Gradually, the through services have been withdrawn. The station, as illustrated in the 1953 photograph, has been largely redeveloped, although it is still possible to trace elements of the older building. Services today comprise largely Pacer-operated workings over the Leeds-York line; these are normally formed of Class 144 units. No 144019 is pictured in the station whilst forming the 13.28 service from Leeds to York. *Author*

Starbeck

Then: Undated

The railway originally arrived at Starbeck in 1848, and the location developed into a busy centre, with lines radiating out to Harrogate, York, Pilmoor, Ripon, Wetherby and Pateley Bridge. The locomotive shed for the Harrogate area was located here; it can be clearly seen in the distance beyond the level crossing as Class J39 0-6-0 No 64861 awaits the road with a freight. In its latter years, Starbeck shed's allocation was mainly Class D49 4-4-0s and 'J39' 0-6-0s. *Kenneth Field*

Now: 20 April 1996

The shed closed in 1959 and, with the exception of the York-Harrogate line via Knaresborough, all the local lines succumbed. Today a frequent DMU service, normally half-hourly, provides a link over the route. The usual rolling stock for the service are the red-liveried Pacer units of Class 144. On this occasion, the 12.04 service from Knaresborough was formed of unit No 144017. On the left, sister unit No 144023 awaits departure for York with the 11.28 service from Leeds. *Author*

Knaresborough

Then: April 1980
This fine station, situated on the Harrogate-York line, opened on its present site in 1851. *Andrew Muckley*

Now: 24 April 1996
The station, which remains open, is still well maintained and sees a frequent DMU service. West Yorkshire PTE-liveried Class 144 No 144017 is shown ready to leave with the 12.05 service to Leeds. The line crosses the impressive viaduct, for which Knaresborough is well known, immediately behind the position from where the photograph was taken. *Author*

Brafferton

Then: 15 August 1961
The line between Knaresborough and Pilmoor opened in two stages: Pilmoor-Boroughbridge in June 1847 and Boroughbridge-Knaresborough in April 1875. By the date of this photograph, passenger services had already been withdrawn — they ceased in September 1950 — and the section from Brafferton to Pilmoor was closed completely at the same time. Traffic was very light at the station when this photograph was taken; York-based Class K1 2-6-0 No 62056 is seen with the daily pick-up freight. *M. Mitchell*

Wormald Green

Then: 30 May 1967
On the date of this photograph a most unusual event took place when the Royal Train, hauled by immaculate Holbeck-based 'Jubilee' No 45562 *Alberta*, visited the Ripon line. The line by this date saw very little traffic and it is believed that HRH Prince Philip was taken to Nidd Bridge for a local visit. The use of steam on the Royal Train, except for ecs working, was exceptional by this time. The train, which was now running as ecs — the Duke of Edinburgh having disembarked for his visit — travelled as far as Ripon to turn round. It is seen passing the closed station at Wormald Green; this had lost its passenger services on 18 June 1962, with freight facilities being withdrawn on 31 August 1964. By this date, No 45562 was also approaching the end of its operational career. *Author*

Ripon

Then: December 1966
In December 1966 the viaduct over the River Ure was still intact and carried the main line, whilst Leeds-Newcastle services continued to operate. Railway services first reached Ripon from Thirsk in January 1848; the line southwards to Weeton opened in two stages later the same year. Here a rake of DMUs forms a Newcastle-Leeds service. *Author*

Now: 13 April 1996
The remaining section of the line, from Knaresborough to Brafferton, was to close completely in October 1964. Today, after more than 30 years, the trackbed can still be clearly identified in both directions, as can the platform edge. The slightly different angle was selected to show the surviving road overbridge. *Author*

Now: 20 April 1996
The former main line from Starbeck to Ripon closed completely in 1969. The trackbed at this point survives and would appear to be used as a public footpath, with nature rapidly taking over. The chimney of the farmhouse in the background is the only point of reference to confirm the location. *Author*

Now: 20 April 1996
Despite being an important route, the line between Harrogate and Northallerton lost its passenger services on 6 March 1967, although, ironically, East Coast main line services were diverted over the route on 1 August the same year due to an accident. A meagre freight service survived until September 1969. After years of traffic chaos in the city, the bypass was opened recently and the 'Now' photograph shows that the river is now crossed by a road rather than a railway bridge. *Author*

Birstwith

Then: 12 March 1964
This was one of five intermediate stations on the branch between Pateley Bridge and Bilton Road Junction. Although passenger services were withdrawn on 2 April 1951, this special was operated from Pateley Bridge just prior to the line's complete closure. A solitary wagon can be seen on the right. *Author*

Pateley Bridge

Then: 12 March 1964
Although the Pateley Bridge branch never boasted a DMU service, on this date a special was run down the line for the benefit of the local school children as it was known that most of them had never travelled on a train. This eight-coach formation took them on a very leisurely schedule to Harrogate and back. As the passenger services over the route had been withdrawn on 2 April 1951 it is easy to see why few of the children had enjoyed train travel. The opportunity was taken to introduce them to railway travel as it was known that freight services over the branch were due to cease later in the year. In the days of steam the branch had been regularly operated for some 33 years by the same Class G5 0-4-4T, No 67253. *Author*

Melmerby

Then: Undated (*circa* mid-1950s)
The line from Ripon and the south split into three at this point, the main line heading for Northallerton, with a secondary route eastwards towards Thirsk and a branch westwards to Masham. The main line, between Harrogate and Northallerton, used to carry such prestige services as the 'Queen of Scots' Pullman and the Newcastle-Liverpool expresses, but these had all been withdrawn or diverted by the time that passenger services were withdrawn in March 1967. One of the 'Hunt' Class D49/2 4-4-0s, No 62745 *The Hurworth* (which survived only until March 1959), is seen passing the North signalbox in charge of a train for Northallerton. As a matter of interest, the Hurworth Hunt takes place around Croft Spa and Northallerton, and the fox emblem can be seen on the top of the nameplate. *J. W. Armstrong*

Now: 20 April 1996
The Pateley Bridge branch was closed
completely on 31 October 1964. Today a
housing estate has been built alongside the
old trackbed and it was difficult to estimate
exactly where I had been standing in 1964
when I took the DMU. I eventually decided
that it was in the back garden of one of the
houses along Birstwith Grange, and I am
grateful to the owner of the house who
allowed me to take this photograph. *Author*

Now: 20 April 1996
Final freight services over the branch were
withdrawn on 31 October 1964. The line
thus achieved its centenary, having been
opened on 1 May 1862. Today, Pateley
Bridge is a busy town and full of tourists
for most of the year. The old goods yard
has been redeveloped into a pleasant
housing estate, with a walkway along the
bank of the River Nidd. *Author*

Now: 10 April 1996
It was very hard to find any evidence that a
railway existed here at all, but with the kind
help of the employees of M. Kettlewell
Transport Ltd, who now own the site, it was
explained that the house on the right of the
photograph had been extended and I was
able to stand in the correct position in the
middle of the company's yard to get the
picture. *Author*

Masham

Then: May 1949
The 7³/₄-mile branch from Melmerby was opened in June 1875. Passenger services were withdrawn from the branch as long ago as December 1930, but the line remained open for freight for a further 33 years. This 1949 photograph shows the layout of the goods yard well.
J. W. Armstrong

Goole

Then: 31 December 1966
Railways first reached the town of Goole on 29 March 1848 with the opening of the Wakefield, Pontefract & Goole Railway (later absorbed by the L&YR). The North Eastern Railway arrived in 1869 with the opening of its line from Staddlethorpe Junction (on the line to Hull) and Thorne (on the GCR line to Grimsby). This allowed for a through Hull-Doncaster service. A second NER line, dating from the first decade of the 20th century, linked Goole with Selby; this line was to lose its passenger services on 15 June 1964 and is now closed completely. English Electric Type 4 (later Class 40) No D391 approaches Goole station from the west.
Author

Staddlethorpe/ Gilberdyke Junction

Then: 6 April 1968
This is the point where the Hull & Selby Railway (opened on 1 July 1840) met the 1869-opened line southwards through Goole to Thorne. The station was known as Staddlethorpe until 1974 when it was rechristened Gilberdyke. An unusual visitor on this occasion was No 4472 *Flying Scotsman* which was working a special that eventually travelled up the line via Bridlington to Scarborough. *Author*

Now: 10 April 1996
Freight services over the Masham branch were withdrawn in December 1963. Nature has completely obliterated the view from the overbridge today, although the station buildings are still occupied as a private house. Some local people told me that the site is due for redevelopment in the near future. *Author*

Now: 22 June 1996
The main line from Doncaster to Hull is still well used and there is an infrequent service from Leeds via Knottingley over the ex-L&YR route. Whilst the docks seem to be busy, there is only a small amount of railway traffic. *Author*

Now: 22 June 1996
The lines through Gilberdyke are still well used, although there has been some rationalisation. The name on the signalbox has changed. Sprinter No 156470 approaches the station on a Doncaster-Hull working at 11.56. This is very much Sprinter territory, the only regular locomotive-hauled workings being the Tilcon limestone and the Saltend tank trains, although there are occasionally other workings to Hull docks. *Author*

Brough

Then: 13 June 1962
This station is situated on the north side of the Humber on the line from Goole to Hull. It is located some 10 miles west of Hull. The Hull & Selby Railway was opened on 1 July 1840. Gresley Class K3 2-6-0 No 61893 heads a freight towards Hull. The train seems to consist mainly of brake vans. At this time the line was very heavily used by freight to and from the port of Hull. *I. S. Carr*

Now: 22 June 1996
One of the West Yorkshire PTE Class 158s, No 158910, enters the station on the 10.34 from Manchester Piccadilly to Hull. The station has become a busy commuter station for Hull, but the track layout has been rationalised over the past 35 years. There is still, however, a signalbox at the east end, which controls the level crossing. *Author*

Withernsea

Then: July 1949

Thompson 'L1' 2-6-4T No 67764, still with British Railways lettering on the tank, is ready to leave with a train to Hull. The station opened on 27 June 1854. The branch was 20¾ miles in length and had 13 intermediate stations (although Sculcoates closed as long ago as June 1912). *Ian Allan Library (K374)*

Now: 23 June 1996

The Withernsea branch lost its passenger services on 19 October 1964 and freight beyond Hedon on 3 May 1965. Much of the trackbed now forms a cycleway (the South Holderness Rail Trail). When I visited the town to take this photograph, it was market day. The old station area is well used, with even the platform awnings still extant. *Author*

Hull Paragon

Then: 11 June 1962
The trackwork on the approach to the station used to be very complicated. Thompson Class B1 4-6-0 No 61289 is pictured backing into the station to work an up King's Cross express. Hull Paragon opened on 8 May 1848, the original terminus being designed by G. T. Andrews; the fine overall roof, which survives today, was completed in 1905. *I. S. Carr*

Now: 22 June 1996
Although the station approach has been simplified and the number of platforms in use has been reduced, Hull Paragon remains an important terminus. West Yorkshire PTE Class 141 No 141115 leaves at 13.50 on a working to Sheffield; this represents a considerable distance for anyone travelling the full journey in these relatively uncomfortable units. The station is still busy with trans-Pennine services as well as those to Sheffield and along the coast to Beverley, Bridlington and Scarborough. *Author*

Hornsea

Then: August 1949
The other branch to head for the coast to the east of Hull was that to Hornsea. This was 15½ miles long and again had 13 intermediate stations. The picture shows one of the Wilson Worsdell-designed North Eastern 4-6-2Ts, designated Class A6 by the LNER, which were built in 1907 and 1908. The locomotive in question, No 69796, was the last of the class to be withdrawn (in March 1953). It is shown having arrived at the station with a relief train from Hull. The Hornsea branch opened on 28 March 1864.
Ian Allan Library (K382)

Now: 22 June 1996
Like the Withernsea branch, the route to Hornsea lost its passenger services on 19 October 1964. Freight services were withdrawn at the same time from Hornsea Bridge to Hornsea Town. The section from Hornsea Bridge to Stonebridge was closed completely from 3 May 1965. Again, much of the Hornsea branch has been converted into a cycleway. The station, which is on the left, is a fine building, particularly when seen from the other side. It appears today to be owned by the local health authority. As can be seen, the site has been redeveloped with houses. *Author*

Beverley

Then: 17 August 1950
Ivatt 2-6-0 No 43052 enters the station with the 10.40am service from Hull to Scarborough. Notice the Minster behind the signalbox. The line opened on 6 October 1846. *Philip Connoley*

Now: 22 June 1996
The station still enjoys an half-hourly service to Hull and an hourly one north to Bridlington. Class 144 No 144006 arrives from Hull. The station building (located behind the photographer) still has an overall roof and is in excellent condition. The signalbox also survives, although the track does appear to be in need of a visit from the weedkiller train. Unfortunately, a new housing development has blocked out the view of the Minster. Until closure of the line on 29 November 1965, it was possible to travel from Beverley, via Market Weighton, to York; the junction was located just to the north of the station. *Author*

The tiled system map of the former North Eastern Railway remains in excellent condition. *Author*

Driffield

Then: April 1973
The lines from Malton, Market Weighton and Beverley used to converge at Driffield, just to the south of the station. Of these, only the route to Hull via Beverley survives. The level crossing to the south of the station was controlled by the Station Gates signalbox and the silhouette of the signalman is clearly visible in this photograph. The railway reached Driffield in 1846 and the station in the town was designed by G. T. Andrews. *Andrew Muckley*

Now: 25 June 1996
The station has altered little in the last 23 years, although some white paint seems to have been liberally applied to the stonework. Automatic barriers now control the crossing. Pacer unit No 142085 arrives at 19.06 with a Bridlington-Hull train. The station building now houses a pub and restaurant. *Author*

Bridlington

Then: Whit Monday 1957

As a railway centre, Bridlington today is but a shadow of its former glory, but both pre- and post-World War 2 it was an extremely busy centre, particularly in the summer months. During the summer season, excursion trains from all over the north of England and beyond would travel to the town. The town boasted its own locomotive shed, which was built in 1892. A typical excursion train of the period, headed by 'B16/2s' Nos 61421 and 61467, leaves the resort for Castleford. Another 'B16' is partially visible as it comes off the shed. *A. M. Ross*

Now: 25 June 1996

The locomotive shed closed in 1958, although the turntable remained available for use after that date. The era of the excursion train is now largely a thing of the past and today Bridlington's staple traffic is the hourly service south to Hull, with limited trains continuing northwards to Filey and Scarborough. West Yorkshire PTE Pacer No 144008 is pictured leaving for Hull on the 18.18 working; it is seen passing weed-strewn sidings. *Author*

Filey Holiday Camp

Then: 6 March 1965
This station, which was a terminus, was situated between Filey itself and Hunmanby. It was accessed by two spurs running off the Scarborough-Hull line, which formed a triangle at Royal Oak North and South junctions. The station was opened on 10 May 1947 to serve the large Butlin's holiday camp, and was therefore used normally only in the summer months. The now preserved 'K1' class 2-6-0 No 62005 is shown about to leave for Scarborough at the head of the 'Whitby Moors' railtour. *Author*

Now: 25 June 1996
The station remained open officially until 26 November 1977, although the last train actually departed on 17 September 1977. The station area was bought by a local farmer who uses the derelict station site for storage. The platforms, of which there were originally four, are still clearly visible. *Author*

Whitby West Cliff

Then: 23 June 1957
This was one of two stations to serve the fishing port of Whitby. The station, located on the Scarborough-Middlesbrough line, was opened in 1883. The Railway Correspondence & Travel Society ran a special to Whitby on this date; motive power was provided by Class D49/1 4-4-0 No 62731 *Selkirkshire* assisted by Class A8 4-6-2 No 69881. The train had to reverse here in order to gain access to the spur down to Whitby Town station. *Author*

Whitby Town

Then: 13 April 1964
The railway reached the town as long ago as 1835 with the opening of the Whitby & Pickering line through the Esk Valley to Grosmont. Over the years Whitby grew into quite a busy railway centre, having a locomotive shed (which closed in 1959) and extensive carriage sidings to deal with summer excursions. In the days when the station could lay claim to several platforms, a Metro-Cammell DMU (later designated Class 101) is pictured ready to leave for Middlesbrough. On the date of this photograph the late Lord Garnock's preserved 'K4' No 3442 *The Great Marquess* was visiting the town with a special for invited guests from Leeds. The special returned by the North Yorkshire Moors line, where filming was undertaken. *Author*

Loftus

Then: mid-1950s
One of the five Standard Class 4MT 2-6-4Ts allocated to Whitby in the mid-1950s, No 80118, is shown at Loftus station heading a local train to Whitby West Cliff and then probably Whitby Town. Passenger services over this route commenced north from here in 1875 and southwards towards Whitby in 1883. *R. J. Buckley*

Now: 25 June 1996
Passenger services north of Whitby West Cliff to Loftus were withdrawn on 3 May 1958, whilst from 12 June 1961 services from Scarborough were diverted over the spur to run into Town station, having reversed at Prospect Hill Junction. Services over the line to Scarborough were withdrawn on 8 March 1965. Thirty-five years after closure, some of the buildings at West Cliff survive, although they now form part of the property of Yorkshire Water. *Author*

Now: 25 June 1996
Two Class 142 Pacer units, Nos 142025 and 142020, are shown ready to depart with the 12.44 service to Middlesbrough from the heavily rationalised station. The rear unit, No 142025, was still in the chocolate and cream livery it received when new to the Western Region. *Author*

Now: 25 June 1996
Passenger services to Loftus from the north ceased on 2 May 1960 (those southwards had succumbed on 5 May 1958) and freight facilities were withdrawn on 12 August 1963. After closure, the line was lifted, but the construction of a major potash mine at Boulby brought new life to the route and the line was reopened in April 1974. The line remains open to serve both the potash mine at Boulby and the British Steel complex at Skinningrove. Occasionally enthusiasts' specials traverse the route. Although the station building survives, the platforms have disappeared and a new bridge has been constructed. *Author*

Sleights

Then: Mid-1950s
This overhead view was taken from the main road bridge above the station and shows a typical country station to advantage. A very dirty Class B1 4-6-0 No 61038 *Blacktail* is entering the station with the 2.10pm stopping train from Whitby Town to Leeds. This service would travel over the now preserved North Yorkshire Moors line via Pickering and Malton. Although the picture is undated, it is probably from the mid-1950s. *A. M. Ross*

Now: 25 June 1996
One platform remains in use and the signalbox still stands, although not used. Two Class 142 Pacers Nos 142020 and 142025 leave on the 11.43 working to Whitby Town. *Author*

Pickering

Then: 13 April 1964

The Whitby & Pickering Railway opened in two stages: from Whitby to Grosmont in June 1835 and thence to Pickering on 26 May 1836. This line was eventually extended to Rillington on the Malton-Scarborough line. Pickering was to become a junction with lines heading west to Gilling and east to Seamer. The train illustrated was a special run from Leeds to Whitby in connection with filming on the North Yorkshire Moors line — note the cameraman on the top of No 3442's tender as the train enters Pickering station from the south. *Author*

Now: 4 April 1996

The line from Rillington to Grosmont lost its passenger services on 8 March 1965, the lines to Seamer (on 5 June 1950) and Pilmoor via Gilling (on 2 February 1953) having lost their passenger services earlier. Although the section north of Pickering remains open as the now preserved North Yorkshire Moors Railway, the line to the south of the town is now closed completely. I had great difficulty in identifying the position to stand, as the scene has changed out of all recognition. There is now a main road and the site behind the trees is a large car park. I decided that the two chimneys on the house under the signal in the 'Then' picture identified the position. *Author*

Gilling

Then: 22 June 1957
The line from Pilmoor to Malton via Gilling opened on 19 May 1853. On 9 October 1871, Gilling became a junction, with the opening of the line to Helmsley. This line was subsequently extended to Kirkbymoorside on 1 January 1874 and to Pickering on 1 April 1875. Passenger services over the line from Gilling to Malton were withdrawn on 1 January 1931 and those from Pilmoor to Pickering on 2 February 1953 (officially; the last trains actually operated on 31 January). At the date of this photograph, the network of lines was intact for freight services. An RCTS special visited the area on 22 June 1957, using Class D49 4-4-0 No 62731 *Selkirkshire*, which is seen taking water. *Author*

Kirkbymoorside

Then: 31 January 1953
This station was situated on the Gilling-Pickering line. It opened between Gilling and Kirkbymoorside on 1 January 1874 and thence to Pickering on 1 January 1875. This photograph, taken on the last day of passenger services, shows that the station already looked semi-derelict. Class D49/1 No 62735 *Westmorland* waits to leave with a train for Pickering. Obviously the local people did not turn out in force to see the last passenger trains — a complete contrast to events a decade later. *J. W. Armstrong*

Battersby

Then: 19 July 1957
Battersby was one of those railway crossroads that the northeast seemed blessed with in large numbers. From the north the line from Middlesbrough came in to join the line from Picton to Grosmont, whilst for good measure there was also the line south to Rosedale. The line to Rosedale was an early casualty, being closed completely in 1928, and by the date of this photograph passenger services westwards to Picton had also been withdrawn (on 14 June 1954). In this photograph Gresley Class V3 2-6-2T No 67646 runs round its train before continuing to Whitby, whilst in the distance Class L1 2-6-4T No 67754 is also running round its train — the 12.5pm service from Whitby to Middlesbrough. *M. Mensing*

Now: 13 April 1996
Freight services over the line from Husthwaite Gate to Amotherby — the section from Pilmoor to Husthwaite Gate having closed in 1962 — and from Gilling to Kirkbymoorside were withdrawn on 10 August 1964. Today the station at Gilling is a private house and I am grateful to the owner for allowing me to take this picture in the back garden. The 'Then' photograph was taken from the station footbridge, the steps of which were used to form the fence in this picture. The platform and canopy still exists, as does the notice to cross the footbridge; the background is, however, very different. *Author*

Now: 4 April 1996
The section between Kirkbymoorside and Pickering was closed completely from 2 February 1953 and freight services between Gilling and Kirkbymoorside ceased on 10 August 1964. The station survives and remains in use. The platform edge for the Pickering side can be clearly seen, although the trackbed has been infilled. *Author*

Now: 13 April 1996
The line westwards from Battersby to Stokesley closed completely on 2 August 1965, leaving the station as a reversal point on the line between Whitby and Middlesbrough. Today the station is an unstaffed halt and the loop remains operational for the occasional loco-hauled train to the coast. The overbridge from which the original photograph was taken has been removed; hence the 'Now' shot was taken from platform level. Only one platform is in use, along with the station buildings. *Author*

Castleton

Then: 6 May 1967

The line opened from Kildale — the first station east from Battersby — to Castleton on 6 April 1858. The line was extended from Kildale to Castleton on 1 April 1861, but it was not until 2 October 1865 that the line was opened between Castleton and Grosmont, thereby giving access to Whitby. Here two trains are seen passing in the station: on the left is a Metro-Cammell DMU (later Class 101) heading for Whitby Town, whilst on the right is Type 3 (later Class 37) No D6778 (now No 37078) at the head of an RCTS special from Bradford. *Author*

Now: 25 June 1996

The Esk Valley line still survives today and now provides Whitby with its only rail connection. The line has a service of around five trains per day. As can be seen, the passing facilities have gone, as has the siding. The 12.44 from Whitby is at the station, formed of Pacer unit No 142020. Run-round facilities still exist at Battersby. *Author*

Neville Hill West

Then: 3 July 1966
This location is at the east end of the famous Marsh Lane cutting and is the junction for the line which goes to Hunslet oil and limestone terminals; this route used to continue through to Beeston Junction, on the ex-Great Northern line from Leeds to Wakefield. The famous Heaton-Red Bank van train is shown leaving, headed by Stockport-allocated 'Britannia' Pacific No 70015 *Apollo* add Newton Heath-based Class 5 No 45200. This combination of motive power was not unusual at this date. *Author*

Now: 18 June 1996
Although there has been some rationalisation of track and the electrification of the line from Leeds to Neville Hill, there remains a junction here. The line continues to serve Hunslet, although it ceased to be a through route with the closure of the line through to Beeston Junction in March 1967. A procession of Pacers and Sprinters pass all day, interspersed with occasional Virgin Cross Country 125s and Class 47s, along with GNER empty stock movements passing to and from Neville Hill. Here Class 158 No 158807 heads east on the 10.12 Manchester Piccadilly-Scarborough service. *Author*

Ledston

Then: 22 April 1967
The station here was situated on the line from Garforth to Castleford. By the date of this photograph passenger services over the route had already been withdrawn, having succumbed on 22 January. Local freight facilities were withdrawn on 22 April 1963, although the pit

was to last longer. Here Leeds Holbeck-based 'Jubilee' No 45593 *Kolhapur* heads a special through the station; at this time the line was still open through to Garforth. *Author*

Now: 18 June 1996
Today little remains of the station and the site of the colliery is now derelict. The track at this date was still *in situ* but was unused. Trains still run to an open cast site about 1/4-mile towards Castleford. This view shows the line heading towards Garforth; the section of line from Allerton Main Colliery to Garforth closed completely on 14 July 1969. *Author*

Burton Salmon

Then: 22 February 1964
The was the point where the lines from Sheffield and Normanton met heading north to York. The layout of the junction is shown to good effect in this photograph of Standard '4MT' No 75043 heading a down goods from Castleford and Normanton. The York-Normanton line opened in 1840 and the section to Knottingley followed on 8 August 1870. Until the completion of the line from Shaftholme Junction to Chaloners Whin in 1871, this route carried GNR trains to York. Burton Salmon station closed on 14 September 1959, although the goods yard remained operational until 3 June 1968. *J. S. Hancock*

Now: 18 June 1996
The Castleford-Burton Salmon section was closed to passenger services on 5 January 1970, but reopened on 7 May 1973. Services were again withdrawn on 4 October 1982. Both routes, however, still remain, although as can be seen, the track layout has been much rationalised.

Loadhaul-liveried Class 60 No 60008 *Gypsum Queen II* heads north on an empty Corby-Lackenby steel train. It will make use of the crossover at Milford Junction. *Author*

Monk Fryston

Then: 10 September 1960
The line through Monk Fryston dates back to 1840. Liverpool (Bank Hall)-allocated unrebuilt 'Patriot' No 45517 approaches Monk Fryston at the head of an evening York-Liverpool express. Monk Fryston station had closed almost exactly one year prior to the date of this photograph, on 14 September 1959. *B. Hartley*

Now: 18 June 1996
The sidings on the right-hand side have gone and the track layout has been simplified, but the signalbox at the top left of the photograph still controls the remaining sidings and the line round to Gascoigne Wood and Selby. Enthusiasts from all over the country now come to this once little-known location to see the endless procession of merry-go-round trains from Gascoigne Wood mine to the power stations at Drax and Eggborough. These trains are hauled by locomotives of Class 56, 58 and 60 as well as the National Power Class 59s. A change from the usual freight traffic is shown by this InterCity 125 set running empty stock northwards. The two power cars were Nos 43155 and 43198. *Author*

Church Fenton

Then: 28 March 1959
This station stands on the line from York to Milford which first opened on 29 May 1839. It became a junction with the opening of the line towards Spofforth on 10 August 1847, but achieved greater significance with the completion of the link to the Leeds-Hull line at Mickleford on 1 April 1869. Until the completion of the Shaftholme Junction-Chaloners Whin Junction line in 1871 East Coast main line services traversed the route. The 3.10pm York-Leeds express is seen at the station headed by Holbeck-allocated Standard Class 5MT No 73171. *M. Mitchell*

Now: 18 June 1996
The Church Fenton-Spofforth-Wetherby line lost its passenger services on 6 January 1964 and the section between Tadcaster and Church Fenton closed completely on 30 November 1966. Services over the lines towards both Leeds and Sheffield, however, survive. The fine station buildings are now history, having been replaced by the usual bus shelters. The station has a regular service over the York-Leeds line and a more irregular one to Sheffield. West Yorkshire PTE Class 158 No 158907 arrives with the 15.13 service from York to Manchester Victoria. *Author*

Chaloners Whin Junction, York
(south)

Then: 10 October 1976
The section of the East Coast main line from York (Chaloners Whin Junction) to Selby opened on 2 January 1871. Not long before the introduction of InterCity 125s to ECML services, an immaculate

Haymarket Class 55 No 55019 *Royal Highland Fusiliers* accelerates the 11.00 Edinburgh Waverley-King's Cross service away from its stop at York. *Author*

Now: 27 September 1996
The York-Selby section of the ECML was replaced by a new main line to the west — the Selby Diversion — as part of the development of the enormous Selby coalfield on 24 September 1983. This photograph, taken from the York ring road, shows how nature has now taken over the route of the ECML at this point. The trackbed is now used as the York-Selby cycle route. *Author*

Dringhouses Yard (York)

Then: 13 April 1964
This picture shows the late Lord Garnock's preserved Gresley 'K4' 2-6-0 No 3442 *The Great Marquess* passing the marshalling yard on the York-Leeds line. The East Coast main line at this point is formed by the two running lines to the right of the locomotive. The locomotive was returning from Whitby at the head of a private charter from Leeds. A Class 03 shunter can be seen in use in the background. *Author*

Now: 27 September 1996
The once busy yards are now closed, no doubt to the relief of the local residents, and today virtually no freight calls regularly at York. Here the 12.53 Blackburn-Lackenby empty steel train 6E41, heads north headed by Class 56 No 56061. *Author*

York

Then: 13 July 1963
The first railways opened in York on 29 May 1839 with the arrival of a branch from the Leeds & Selby Railway at Milford. From these beginnings, York grew into a major railway centre. The line north to Darlington opened on 30 March 1841, that to Scarborough on 7 July 1845, that to Market Weighton on 4 October 1847 and that to Knaresborough on 30 October 1848. The link to Selby, which was to form part of the East Coast main line, opened on 2 January 1871. The original station was built within the city walls, but a new station was opened in 1841. The current station was built between 1874 and 1877. It had 13 platforms, with an additional three being added later. This view, taken of the bay platforms at the north end of the station used by services to the coast, shows Class B1 No 61360 ready to leave with the 3.35pm service to Whitby. This train conveyed through coaches from London King's Cross. On the right Class B16/2 No 61438 awaits departure with the 3.40pm service to Hull; this train will travel via the now long-abandoned route via Stamford Bridge and Market Weighton. *J. M. Rayner*

Now: 27 September 1996
The fine overall roof still stands and is still overlooked by the station hotel. The bay platforms have, however, succumbed and been converted into the main station car park. The rest of the station has changed very little over the past 33 years, with the exception of some rationalisation and the electrification of the ECML. *Author*

Easingwold

Then: 22 June 1957
Technically speaking, the Easingwold Railway is outside the terms of reference for this book, as the line remained independent through to closure. However, as it was operated by North Eastern locomotives for many years, I thought that it was worth including. Opened on 25 July 1891, the 2½-mile branch linked the town of Easingwold with the East Coast main line at Alne. Before World War 2 there were nine passenger services per day, but this was reduced to three after the war, and passenger services ceased to operate completely on 29 November 1948. The line remained open thereafter for freight only. Six months before final closure, the Railway Correspondence & Travel Society (West Riding Branch) operated a special using Class J71 0-6-0T No 68246 and open wagons. The train is seen at the terminus. *Author*

Malton

Then: August 1957
This was an important junction on the York-Scarborough line, which opened on 7 July 1845. A link from the this line was made into the Gilling-Malton-Driffield route, which opened on 19 May 1853. During the August Bank Holiday of 1957, Newton Heath-based Class 5 No 45154 *Lanarkshire Yeomanry* passes with an excursion from Harrogate to Scarborough. The locomotive was apparently standing in for a failed Starbeck-based locomotive. The town's locomotive shed is visible on the left with a local Class J27, No 65827, present. *A. M. Ross*

Now: 25 June 1996
The line between York and Scarborough remains open, although the level of holiday and excursion traffic has declined significantly. The Gilling-Malton-Driffield route is, however, no more. Local services over the Gilling-Malton section were withdrawn on 1 January 1931 (although holiday services continued to traverse the route, with a reversal at Malton, until 1963). Passenger services to Driffield were withdrawn on 5 June 1950 and the line closed completely from Malton to Driffield on 20 October 1958. The section from Malton to Amotherby closed completely on 19 October 1964. All traces of the shed have now gone and the sidings on the left see very little traffic. All passenger trains now use the one platform. Services over the route are still frequent, but are almost entirely worked by either Pacers or Sprinters, whilst locomotive-hauled trains are rare. West Yorkshire PTE No 144004 is leaving on the 10.38 service to York. *Author*

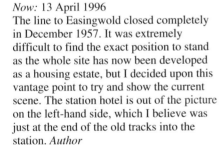

Now: 13 April 1996
The line to Easingwold closed completely in December 1957. It was extremely difficult to find the exact position to stand as the whole site has now been developed as a housing estate, but I decided upon this vantage point to try and show the current scene. The station hotel is out of the picture on the left-hand side, which I believe was just at the end of the old tracks into the station. *Author*

Tollerton

Then: 6 August 1961

The external condition in the early 1960s of some of the famous Gresley 'A4' Pacifics was not all that good, particularly in the case of those allocated to Gateshead (52A) shed, as witnessed by this photograph of No 60020 *Guillemot*. This locomotive spent its entire career from 1937 to 1964 allocated to the Newcastle area sheds of Gateshead and Heaton. It is shown here on a hot summer's day heading the up 'Heart of Midlothian' express. *Author*

Now: 13 April 1996

Tollerton station lost its freight facilities on 6 September 1965 and the station itself closed on the following 1 November. All signs of the station's northbound platform have now gone and today's picture, taken of a Class 158 unit No 158812 on a Middlesbrough-Manchester service, looks very different with electrification. The background also looked different and caused some confusion until a conversation with a local farmer confirmed that some of the fields had been relandscaped. *Author*

Pilmoor

Then: 16 August 1959
In the late 1940s and 1950s this was a favourite place for me to go and watch trains. You could see and hear trains, especially expresses headed by 'V2s', sometimes for six or seven minutes. On this occasion Class B16/3 No 61439 heads north with an express freight. Note the earthworks being carried out on the left-hand side for the building of the fourth (up slow) line through to York from Pilmoor. If one looks carefully in the background, just beyond the end of the train, the crossover can be seen for the junction with the line towards the east coast via Gilling and Pickering. This route was regularly used — until 1962 when a service derailed and destroyed the junction — for summer services from Scotland and the northeast to Scarborough. The main line through Pilmoor opened on 4 January 1841 for freight and 30 January 1841 for passenger services. The line west from Pilmoor to Boroughbridge opened on 17 June 1847 and that east to Gilling on 19 May 1853. *Author*

Now: 13 April 1966
This location has been ruined photographically by electrification. Brand new EMU No 365528, built at the now closed York Carriage Works, was on trial in its Network SouthEast livery prior to delivery. Compare the tree-free embankment in the 'Then' photograph with the current scene. Passenger services between Pilmoor and Knaresborough were withdrawn on 25 September 1950; at the same time the line closed completely between Brafferton and Pilmoor. The line to Gilling lost its passenger services (with the exception of summer traffic) on 2 February 1953. The section between Pilmoor and Husthwaite Gate closed completely on 10 September 1962. Pilmoor station itself had closed on 5 May 1958 and lost its freight facilities on 14 September 1959. *Author*

Northallerton

Then: 5 March 1961
The main line station can be seen in the right background. There were once platforms at this location, evidence of which can be seen by the 50mph speed restriction sign, but these were closed in 1901. A Thornaby-allocated 'Austerity' 2-8-0 No 90461 heads south with a loaded steel train from the Middlesbrough area. In the background is the small locomotive shed, which was to close in March 1963. In 1959 the shed had an allocation of seven locomotives and three were on shed on this occasion. One of the trio was Class K1 No 62044, which was used on the Wensleydale freight service. *Author*

Now: 9 August 1996
The lines are still in use today, helping to avoid crossover operation with the East Coast main line. There is nothing left to suggest that there were once a yard and a shed at the location. *Author*

Leeming Bar

Then: Undated
This station is located six miles from Northallerton on the Wensleydale line. This route was opened from Northallerton to Bedale in 1848. Passenger services through to Hawes ceased on 26 April 1954, but freight facilities continued to be provided at this station until 1 November 1965. The line continued in use for limestone traffic to Redmire until 1992, when it was mothballed. *Ian Allan Library*

Now: 9 August 1996
The goods shed still stands, although the yard area appears to be unused today. The line still survives and has now found a new use: it was reopened for Ministry of Defence traffic on 10 April 1996. *Author*

Leyburn

Then: 25 April 1964
Situated at the heart of Wensleydale, the market town of Leyburn was added to the railway map in May 1856 when the line was extended from Bedale. Passenger services survived for 98 years, before the through service from Northallerton to Garsdale ceased on 26 April 1954. The last working Class B16 4-6-0 No 61435 is shown heading towards Hawes on an RCTS special after the line had closed for regular passenger services. *Author*

Now: 9 August 1996
The line remained opened as far as Redmire for limestone traffic until December 1992. Following mothballing, the line has been much in the news over the last few years, as there has been a very active preservation group campaigning to reopen the line. As yet they have not succeeded, but the line has reopened for use by the MoD. The reopening required a great deal of engineering work, which was a joint venture between the MoD and Railtrack. The first train ran on 10 April 1996, but not without some technical problems. Four months after the reopening, the state of the track shows that the new traffic is only irregular. *Author*

Now: 13 April 1996
The Picton-Battersby line lost its passenger services on 14 June 1954, at which time the Esk Valley trains, which had historically linked Stockton with Whitby, were diverted to run to Middlesbrough. Freight services between Picton and Stokesley were withdrawn on 1 December 1958. Today, if one travels around on the motorways, especially in the north of England, you cannot fail to notice articulated lorries bearing the name 'Prestons of Potto'. It puzzled for some time as to where exactly Potto was. I now know, as the company's head office is situated just off to the right in this photograph and one of their warehouses can be seen in the background. The station house is now privately owned and is in splendid external condition. *Author*

Now: 9 August 1996
Freight services over the Richmond branch were withdrawn on 2 August 1965 and passenger services were to follow on 3 March 1969. It was not possible to stand in exactly the same position as in the 'Then' photograph, without demolishing the house owners' well-kept flower beds, so I took this view from the other platform. As can be seen, the station has now been converted into a very pleasant private house. *Author*

Now: 9 August 1996
Apart from the electrification of the ECML, little has changed fortunately to the appearance of this fine station with the exception of some track rationalisation. I intended to wait for a train to arrive in the up platform, but minutes after taking this photograph a violent thunderstorm broke, so I decided to return to the car, keep dry and head for home. *Author*

Shildon

Then: Undated (late 1950s)
This picture was taken looking east from the road bridge just before Shildon station at the point where the lines used to branch off to serve the wagon works. Shildon is situated on part of the original Stockton & Darlington Railway, and the route between Shildon and Darlington follows the alignment of that historic route; to the west of Shildon to Bishop Auckland a deviation route was built later to replace the original S&D line. Ivatt 2-6-0 No 43129 heads towards Bishop Auckland with a passenger working as a diesel shunter waits for its next duty in the yard. *J. W. Armstrong*

Now: 5 May 1996
The changes here have been dramatic. All that is left today are the main line and two little used sidings. The line to the works — which closed on 29 June 1984 — have been long disconnected. This was the site of the stands erected for the thousands of people to watch the famous 'Rocket 150' procession from Shildon to Darlington in September 1975. Shuttle trains between the works and the sidings ran during the celebrations with most unusual motive power for this part of the country, including ex-GWR 4-6-0 *Raveningham Hall* and ex-LBSCR 0-6-0T 'Terrier' *Fenchurch. Author*

Bishop Auckland

Then: 10 April 1965
This was a busy triangular station, with lines heading out to Barnard Castle, Wearhead, Crook, Consett, Durham and Darlington. The town had its own locomotive shed, which provided motive power on all the routes. On this occasion, the preserved 'K4' 2-6-0 No 3442 *The Great*

Marquess (then owned by the late Lord Garnock) was being turned on the triangle, having visited the Weardale line, before heading back to Durham. It is shown at the east end of the triangle taking water. *Author*

Now: 4 May 1996
Major changes have taken place, with all the lines, save the passenger link to Darlington and the now mothballed route to Eastgate, having closed. Much of the site has been redeveloped into the ubiquitous shopping centre. The single-car Class 153 No 153304 is shown arriving at 11.25 from Darlington. There were a good number of passengers waiting to make the trip back to Darlington at 11.39. A wide-angle lens was used to record the 'Now' scene, which gives a slightly different perspective to that of the 'Then' shot, taken with a standard lens. *Author*

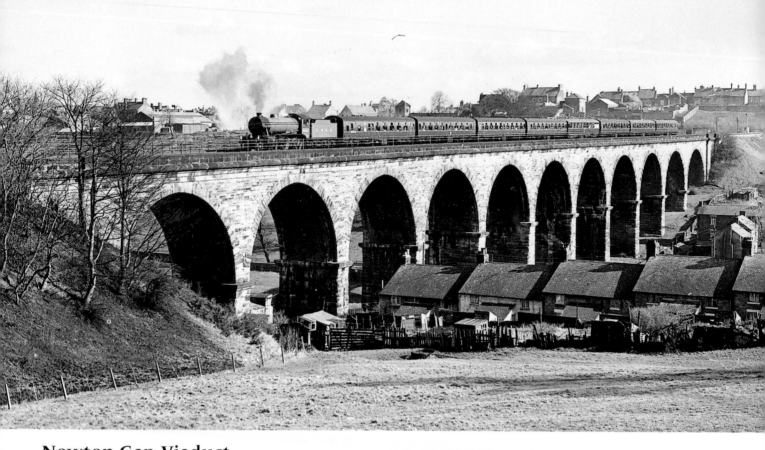

Newton Gap Viaduct

Then: 10 April 1965
This viaduct, on the line between Bishop Auckland and Leamside, was built in 1857. It was 830ft long and 105ft high. Here the preserved 'K4' No 3442 is seen passing over the viaduct with a special. *Author*

Now: 4 May 1996
The line from Bishop Auckland to Leamside closed during the 1960s and in 1972 Durham County Council bought the viaduct and opened a footpath across it in 1974. In the mid-1980s the county council decided that there was a need for a new river crossing for the A689 road and that the viaduct could be reused for that purpose. Work was started on the conversion in September 1993 and the new road opened in July 1995, having cost £4.25 million. Although it is to be regretted that cars rather than trains now use the bridge, the conversion has at least ensured the survival of the viaduct. *Author*

Frosterley

Then: 10 April 1965
A Railway Correspondence & Travel Society special, organised by the society's West Riding branch and headed by the preserved 'K4' No 3442, is shown passing the impressive station building as it headed west through the valley as far as St Johns. The railway opened to Frosterley on 3 August 1847, although it was to be a further 15 years before the line was extended to Stanhope and further into the Wear Valley. Passenger services over the line were withdrawn on 29 June 1953. *Author*

Now: 4 May 1996
The line through Frosterley remained in use for cement traffic to Eastgate until the early 1990s. The line is currently mothballed, although a number of specials have operated over it since closure. These have been operated by a group which is investigating the possibility of reopening the line as a preserved operation. The station house looked to be in excellent condition. *Author*

Stanhope

Then: 26 June 1953
The line from Frosterley to Stanhope opened on 22 October 1862 and, until the opening of the line to Wearhead in 1895, Stanhope was the terminus of the line. Shortly before passenger services were withdrawn, Class J21 0-6-0 No 65061 enters the station heading west with a service for Wearhead. With only two people on the platform, it would appear that the local population was not showing much interest in the last days of the line's passenger services. The 'J21s' were regular performers over the route for many years. *A. B. Crompton*

Now: 4 May 1996
Passenger services over the Wearhead line were withdrawn from 29 June 1953, although the line remained open for freight. After 1968 services ran only as far as the cement works at Eastgate, but even this traffic has ceased and the line is now mothballed. Apart from the considerable work undertaken on the up platform, the station provided a fairly dismal picture in early May 1996, although it has been suggested that Stanhope would be the headquarters of the preservation society if and when the project goes ahead. *Author*

Eastgate

Then: 10 April 1965
A further view of the RCTS (West Riding Branch) special sees the preserved 'K4' passing the station at Eastgate. The line beyond Stanhope, via Eastgate to Wearhead opened on 21 October 1895. When this picture was taken, passenger services had long ceased, being withdrawn on 29 June 1953. The line beyond the cement works, which were located about a further half-mile to the west, was closed in three

stages: From Wearhead to St John's Chapel on 2 January 1961; from St John's Chapel to Westgate on 1 November 1965 and from Westgate to the cement works at Eastgate on 1 July 1968. Note the Blue Circle cement wagons together with the cement lorry and the old Austin A55 car in the yard. *Author*

Now: 4 May 1996
The line to the cement works is now mothballed, although there are hopes that the route will be preserved. Renovation work appeared to be taking place on the station house and the goods shed was still standing. Ironically, the railway wagons once used for the cement traffic were still present at the cements works, although unused. *Author*

Wearhead

Then: Undated; probably *circa* 1950
The line beyond Stanhope to Wearhead opened on 21 October 1895. Here Class J21 0-6-0 No 65089 awaits departure from the terminus with a train for Darlington.
J. W. Armstrong

Barnard Castle

Then: September 1956
This used to be a busy centre, with lines heading for Kirkby Stephen, Middleton-in-Teesdale, Bishop Auckland and Darlington. One of the features was the fine rake of signals at the east junction. Standard Class 3MT 2-6-2T No 82027 is ready to leave for the westbound journey over Stainmore, whilst Class A8 4-6-2T No 69874 waits to leave with a train for Middleton-in-Teesdale.
Ian Allan Library (K3208)

Middleton-in-Teesdale

Then: September 1956
The short branch to Middleton-in Teesdale left the main Stainmore line at Barnard Castle. The line opened on 12 May 1868. Here Class A8 4-6-2T No 69874 waits to depart from the terminus with a train for Bishop Auckland. The small engine shed can be seen to the left of the photograph, although it would appear to be out of use by this date. *Ian Allan Library (K3209)*

Now: 4 May 1996
Passenger services over the route were withdrawn on 29 June 1953 and the section of line between St John's Chapel and Wearhead was closed completely from 2 January 1961. There was very little left to identify the location when I took this picture, except for the top of the goods shed on the left-hand side. The area would appear to have been taken over by the local vet, with new buildings erected to house the animals. *Author*

Now: 5 May 1996
The Stainmore line closed on 22 January 1962, whilst passenger services over the Middleton-in-Teesdale branch ceased on 30 November 1964 with freight ending on 5 April 1965. Over the past 30 years the presence of the railway in Barnard Castle has been gradually obliterated and an industrial estate now stands where the railway once ran. My thanks must go to the local resident who helped me to pinpoint the location. *Author*

Now: 4 May 1996
Passenger services over the branch were withdrawn on 30 November 1964 and freight followed on 5 April the following year. The station site has now become a caravan park. It was difficult to identify the correct location to take the photograph, but the station building can be seen behind the tree on the right-hand side. *Author*

Bowes

Then: Undated
The station at Bowes was situated to the east of the summit at Stainmore. The date on the stonework between the locomotive and the gas lamp reads '1858' — a good indication of the period of the line's construction. Class J25 No 5662 heads east through the station. Although this photograph is undated, the fact that the locomotive retains its LNER number would suggest a date just after World War 2. *J. W. Armstrong*

Now: 5 May 1996
The line through Bowes closed completely on 22 January 1962. Unlike many of the other stations on the line, time has not been kind to the station buildings here, as evidenced by this scene of dereliction. The upgraded A66 trunk road, part of which uses the trackbed of the closed railway, is visible on the extreme left. *Author*

Barras

Then: circa 1950

The line across the Pennines between Barnard Castle and Tebay was authorised in 1857 with work starting later the same year The 35-mile stretch from Barnard Castle to Tebay opened for mineral traffic on 4 July 1861 and to passenger services on 7 August 1861. Originally single track (but with an expectation of future doubling), the section between Stainmore Summit and Barras was doubled in 1874. Here one of the ex-NER Class J21 0-6-0s, which monopolised services on the route for many years, is seen leaving the station with a service for Darlington. There does appear to be a passenger or two on the platform, but passenger receipts must have been low in this isolated area. Barras used to be the highest main line station in Britain, and snow blockages on the line were frequent. These were graphically portrayed in the film *Snowdrift at Bleathgill* filmed in 1947. *J. W. Armstrong*

Now: 5 May 1996

Passenger services on the Stainmore line were withdrawn on 22 January 1962 and freight over the Stainmore line ceased at the same time. Today the station house is occupied, and the platform edges can still be seen. *Author*

Stainmore Summit

Then: 16 August 1958
This bleak and wild location was 1,370ft above sea level, a fact which was shown on a large sign erected in about 1930. The A66 road can be seen in the background; in the winter, this was always one of the first trans-Pennine routes to be blocked. Here two of the batch of BR Standard Class 2MTs allocated new to the line are ready to leave the summit bound for Bishop Auckland. The leading locomotive, No 78017, had acted as banker to No 78013 up the gradient from Kirkby Stephen. *Author*

Belah Viaduct

Then: 20 January 1962
Built in 1859 to the design of Thomas Bouch, who was also the designer of the ill-fated first Tay railway bridge, this superb structure was 1,040ft long and 196ft high. It cost a total of £31,630 to construct. The 'Stainmore Limited' special, which ran on 20 January 1962, became the last train to cross the viaduct when it returned to Darlington. Standard Class 3 2-6-0 No 77003 piloted Standard Class 4 2-6-0 No 76049 on the train, and the pair are seen on the outward journey to Tebay coasting across the viaduct. *Author*

Kirkby Stephen East

Then: 6 August 1960
Work started on the South Durham & Lancashire Union line on 25 August 1857, when the first sod was cut at Kirkby Stephen. One hundred and three years later a summer Saturdays Only South Shields-Blackpool train rolls into the station after coming over Stainmore Summit. It is headed by BR Standard Class 4MT No 76024 and Ivatt '4MT' 2-6-0 No 43129 and will continue to Tebay to join the West Coast main line. Kirkby Stephen was the main centre of the route and had a yard and a motive power shed. *Derek Cross*

Now: 5 May 1996
The final train ran on 20 January 1962 and the line over the summit was quickly dismantled. The area of the trackbed is now little more than rubble with the immediate surrounding area nothing more than a bog. The A66 road still runs by in the background with a virtually unending procession of heavy goods vehicles. If the proposal to rebuild a railway back to Stainmore ever happens, it will be a miracle, but it won't be the first time that railway preservationists have performed miracles. *Author*

Now: 5 May 1996
Despite many protests, the magnificent structure was demolished in late 1963, some 18 months after the complete closure of the line. The surrounding scenery has changed little over the past 34 years. The shell of the signalbox still stands at the Kirkby Stephen end of the viaduct and plans exist to reopen the line from Kirkby Stephen to Stainmore. Could this be yet another miracle in the railway preservation movement? *Author*

Now: 5 May 1996
The last through passenger train, an RCTS special, ran from Darlington to Tebay on 20 January 1962. The section between Appleby and Kirkby Stephen was retained for freight traffic to Merrygill Quarry, but the line was closed beyond Warcop on 31 October 1974. This view is looking towards Stainmore Summit and shows that the site of the yard is now a well laid out caravan park. On the other side of the bridge, the former station site is now in industrial use. There are proposals for a railway to run to here again and on up to Stainmore Summit, but there will obviously be some problems in passing through this location. *Author*

Ravenstonedale

Then: 20 January 1962
This was one of two intermediate stations on the line between Tebay and Kirkby Stephen East and was located to the west of the point at which the former NER route passed under the ex-Midland Railway Settle-Carlisle line. In this illustration the crew of Standard Class 3MT No 77003, which was piloting Standard Class 4MT No 76049, are preparing to change the tablet for the last time with a westbound train as the RCTS-sponsored special heads towards Tebay. Passenger services over the Tebay-Kirkby Stephen section had been withdrawn from 1 December 1952, but freight services were to survive for a further decade. This train, the 'Stainmore Limited', was the last to traverse the route before closure. *Author*

Now: 10 June 1996
The line closed officially from 22 January 1962. Although the goods shed has been demolished, the station survives as a house and the platform edge remains to remind visitors that this was once an important trans-Pennine railway route. The road overbridge also survives, but is hidden by the bushes. *Author*

Leadgate

Then: 18 March 1964
This station was situated just to the east of Consett on the route which was heavily used for the iron ore traffic from Tyne Dock. On this occasion Class 9F 2-10-0 No 92099 was being banked by 'Austerity' 2-8-0 No 90434. This line had its origins in the Stanhope & Tyne Railroad, which opened between Stanhope and Annfield on 15 May 1834 and thence to South Shields on 10 September 1834. Much of the line was originally worked by inclined planes, but in 1886 and 1887 deviation routes were opened to obviate the need for four of the planes. Passenger services over the line from Blackhill via Consett and Leadgate to Birtley were withdrawn on 23 May 1955. The colliery at Leadgate can just be seen in the background. *Author*

Now: 11 June 1996
Following the closure of the steelworks at Consett, the Consett-Washington line was closed completely in the early 1980s. The only reminders from the 'Then' picture are the wall in the foreground and the Jolly Drovers public house, which appeared to be flourishing. A new roundabout has been built and the embankment has been removed. *Author*

Deerness Valley Junction

Then: 8 August 1966
There used to be a complex network of lines at this location, just to the south of Durham near Relly Mill. 'Jubilee' No 45593 *Kolhapur* was not the usual motive power in this part of the country, but on this occasion it was at the head of the Heaton-Manchester Red Bank van train. This view is taken from the east side of the East Coast main line looking north, and shows the complex network to good effect. Behind the train is the line to Bishop Auckland, whilst the Consett-Bridge House lines passes underneath with the connecting spur in the background. In its heyday, this must have been one of the busiest railway locations in the northeast. *I. S. Carr*

South Pelaw Junction

Then: 1 September 1961
This location was well recorded over the years by photographers. Only a mile or so from the East Coast main line, north of Chester-le-Street, one was able to observe the ex-North Eastern Class Q7 0-8-0s battling with the ore trains from Tyne Dock to Consett until their replacement by the Standard Class 9Fs for the final years of steam operation. The complex layout, with signalbox, is shown to good effect in this view of 'Q7' No 63460 (now preserved on the North Yorkshire Moors Railway) heading for Consett with a rake of flat wagons. The lines to the right headed for Stella Gill coal yard. *A. R. Butcher*

Pelaw

Then: 23 July 1966
Situated on the south side of the Tyne to the east of Newcastle, Pelaw was an important junction in steam days. The lines to the left headed towards Tyne Dock, those in the centre to Sunderland and those on the right headed for Leamside. This last-named line was often used as a diversionary route off the East Coast main line to the south. Here Class 9F 2-10-0 No 92097 takes the Boldon Colliery line with a Consett-Tyne Dock empties working. This train had been diverted from its usual route via West Boldon and Washington. *I. S. Carr*

Now: 29 June 1996
As can be seen, the complex network of routes has shrunk, so that only the East Coast main line still survives. The Consett-Relly Mill Junction line had lost its passenger services as early as 1 May 1939, but the line remained open for freight until 3 October 1966. The Durham-Waterhouses line lost its passenger services on 29 October 1951, with freight following on 5 April 1964. Passenger services over the Bishop Auckland-Durham line ceased on 4 May 1964. Freight services over the Bishop Auckland route lasted until 5 August 1968. The alignment of the main line has been altered to help ease the original sharp curve. The 14.00 Edinburgh-King's Cross service heads south. *Author*

Now: 29 June 1996
Following the closure of the Consett steel works, freight traffic over the line to Consett dwindled and the line closed. The track was lifted in 1985 and the route is now used for one of the new long-distance cycle paths promoted by Sustrans. Looking east today, there is little to indicate that this used to be a busy railway junction. *Author*

Now: 29 June 1996
Today the scene has changed. The area to the right is now occupied by the units of the Tyne & Wear Metro. The other lines, however, survive, although their functions may have changed. The line to the left now serves the Shell oil terminal at Jarrow, the lines in the middle still head to Sunderland (over which a frequent service still operates), whilst the line to the right heads towards Wardley. Metro unit No 4054 is seen heading outbound towards South Shields; the unit will cross over the Sunderland line in the distance before running parallel with the freight-only line towards Jarrow. *Author*

Tyne Dock

Then: 18 March 1964
The Tyne Dock-Consett iron ore trains were one of the most spectacular freight operations in the country. In the latter days of operation BR Standard Class 9F 2-10-0s, of which 10 were allocated to Tyne Dock shed for the duties, blasted their way up to the steel works at Consett on gradients as steep as 1 in 35 with 500-ton trains. On this occasion No 92066 prepares to leave with a loaded train from under the massive loading bunkers. *Author*

Now: 29 June 1996
The Consett Iron Co dated back as far as 1864, but the steel works were to close completely in 1983, being dismantled thereafter and destroying the industrial skyline of Consett (and the livelihood of many of its residents). The steam-operated Tyne Dock-Consett trains ran for the last time on 19 November 1966, when No 92063 officiated. Today, Tyne Dock is still rail connected, but in comparison with the past the lines are little used. Fortunately, on my visit, one of the security guards had worked at the docks for more than 30 years and was able to advise me where to stand to get this picture. As is evident, there was little else to guide me as to the location. *Author*

Sunderland

Then: 22 March 1961
The first significant railway to reach Sunderland was the Durham &
Sunderland which introduced a goods service in 1836. Subsequent to
that, the city developed as a major railway centre, but it was not until
1879 that lines to the north and south of the River Wear were connected.
Class A2/3 Pacific No 60515 heads the 12.5pm Newcastle-Colchester
train out of the station. A Metro-Cammell DMU (later Class 101) can be
seen in the background. *D. J. Dippie*

Now: 29 June 1996
This rather cramped location is still in existence, although the
surrounding buildings have been dramatically modernised. The
replacement signalbox seems to have suffered from the local graffiti
artists. *Author*

Hart Junction

Then: 26 August 1966
Hart station was to the rear of the photographer and was located just to the north of Hartlepool. The first railway to reach Hartlepool was that from Haswell, which opened in 1835. This was followed in November 1840 by the opening of the line to Stockton and in 1905 by the opening of the line along the coast to Sunderland. Passenger services over the old route between Hartlepool and Ferryhill ceased on 9 June 1952. Hart station itself closed on 31 August 1953 and lost its freight facilities on 2 March 1959. The 12 noon Newcastle-Colchester train, headed by English Electric Type 4 (later Class 40) No D343 overtakes Ivatt 2-6-0 No 43057 on a train from the Durham collieries. *John H. Bird*

Wellfield

Then: 2 May 1964
This location was on the inland route from Sunderland to Teesside, which opened for mineral services from Sunderland to Haswell on 5 July 1836 and for passenger services on the following 30 August. Passenger services finished on 9 June 1952 on the section from Murton southwards to Haswell and Hartlepool; the northern section of the line, from Sunderland to Pittington saw passenger services withdrawn on 5 January 1953. Although long-closed, the station and platforms were still pretty well intact when this RCTS special called. It is interesting that it was hauled by 'Q7' 0-8-0 No 63460, which along with the rest of the class had been withdrawn in November and December 1962. Pending preservation, the locomotive was put aside in Darlington Works, but was reinstated specially for this tour before being sent to Stratford, London. Eventually it arrived on the North Yorkshire Moors Railway, where it has been restored to working order. *Author*

Billingham

Then: 14 April 1955
This station was situated on the Stockton-Hartlepool line. The first line to serve the area was, however, the mineral line of the Clarence Railway, which was extended to Billingham and Norton Junction (for Stockton) on 29 October 1833. This route carried passenger traffic from a later date, although these trains were withdrawn south of Haverton Hill on 11 September 1939 and withdrawn completely (save for some workmen's trains) between Billingham and Haverton Hill on 14 June 1954. Billingham became a junction with the opening of the Stockton & Hartlepool Railway to freight in late 1840 and to passenger traffic in February 1841. Leeds (Neville Hill)-allocated Class A3 No 60074 *Harvester* passes the station. *A. M. Bowman*

Now: 29 June 1996
Although the original route is now closed, the 1905 coastal line to Sunderland is still open and sees a regular service of Pacer and Sprinter units. However, no trains were due for some time when this photograph was taken, and freight traffic is now also sparse. *Author*

Now: 29 June 1996
The line has closed completely and only the road bridge remains. The trackbed is now a footpath and a small pond seems to have appeared. *Author*

Now: 29 June 1996
The original Billingham station closed on 7 November 1966, but was replaced by a new station half-a-mile to the east. However, as can be seen, evidence of the old station in the form of signalbox, semaphore signals, footbridge and crossing still remains. The line towards Haverton Hill also survives, providing access to the many rail-served industrial sites on the north side of the River Tees. Class 156 No 156454 heads south towards Stockton. *Author*

Thornaby

Then: September 1964

As can be seen, the station buildings here, which were situated on an island platform, were impressive. Stanier 2-6-4T No 42477, allocated to Darlington at the time, passes with a train from Middlesbrough to Darlington. The station is situated on the Middlesbrough extension of the Stockton & Darlington Railway; this line was authorised on 23 May 1828 and opened on 27 December 1830. Between Stockton and Thornaby the railway had to cross the River Tees; as a result of restrictions within the original act, the first railway bridge at this point was built as a suspension bridge. This, however, proved unsuccessful and was replaced by a new bridge in 1841. A third bridge, built in 1907, utilised parts of the 1841 structure. *Peter H. Pegg*

Now: 29 June 1996

The station is still open today, although the buildings have been reduced to no more than bus shelters. The size of the island platform can be clearly seen. Whilst Teesside is still an industrial area, there are more open spaces around than in the past. Class 153 No 153378 calls at 18.59 *en route* to Darlington. *Author*

Low Fell Junction

Then: 26 June 1964

Although Tyne Dock's allocation of Class 9Fs were primarily based at the shed for use on the Consett iron ore trains, they did have other duties in the region. One of the class, No 92062, is seen pulling out of the goods yards at Bensham with an oil train destined for Consett. On the right is the East Coast main line, whilst the lines on the left provided access to the line westwards to Carlisle. *M. Dunnett*

Middlesbrough

Then: 6 May 1962
Railways reached Middlesbrough on
27 December 1840 with the opening of the
extension of the Stockton & Darlington
Railway from Stockton. The line was
extended to Redcar on 4 June 1846 and to
Guisborough on 25 February 1854. The
present station at Middlesbrough dates from
December 1877, when it was provided with
an overall roof. This was, however,
destroyed during a German raid in August
1942. A rare visitor to the area was
Holbeck-based 'Jubilee' No 45562 *Alberta*
which was at the head of an RCTS special
from Bradford Exchange. *Author*

Now: 29 June 1996
Although the station has lost its centre road,
little else has changed over 30 years. The
station is now brighter than it used to be,
with attractive flower tubs. The lines to
Stockton and Redcar survive, as does the
line towards Guisborough which now forms
the start of the Whitby branch. Class 153
No 153304 calls at 18.30 with a train for
Redcar. *Author*

Now: 29 June 1996
The layout is now simplified and there is no
connection between the line towards
Carlisle and the East Coast main line at this
point. An InterCity 125, with power cars
Nos 43111 and 43107, heads south at 12.02
on the 07.55 Aberdeen-King's Cross
service. Access to the Royal Mail depot at
Low Fell is gained by the line towards
Carlisle. *Author*

Newcastle Central

Then: 25 August 1960
This must be one of the best recorded locations in the north of England. The view of the station taken from the 'keep tower' gives an excellent perspective of this complex layout at the north end of Central station. The up 'Queen of Scots' is shown arriving headed by Class A2/3 Pacific No 60517 *Ocean Swell*. Note the electrified lines on the right-hand side of the picture, and the electric units in the station.
I. S. Carr

Now: 29 June 1996
The skyline has altered dramatically, but not as much as the trackwork visible in the foreground. As is so common these days, the operational part of the station has been significantly reduced and much of the space converted to provide additional car parking accommodation. Class 158 No 158803 is leaving the station with a service to Liverpool. *Author*

Monkseaton

Then: 10 February 1967
Electrification on Tyneside goes back to 1904. The main contractors for the original rolling stock, which was built at York, were British Thomson-Houston (BTH). In 1937 articulated rolling stock built by Metro-Cammell arrived and one of these units is pictured leaving the station. The articulated units were largely replaced by BR in 1955 with stock almost identical to the Southern Region's '2EPBs'. The lines were de-electrified from 1963, with the most modern stock transferred to the Southern Region. The process of de-electrification continued and the last Tyneside electrics operated on 17 June 1967 when all the ex-LNER stock still in service was withdrawn. *K. Pringle*

Now: 11 June 1996
After a period of DMU operation, the line through Monkseaton was transferred to the new Tyne & Wear Metro with conversion taking place. The first section of the new Metro opened in August 1980. One of the 90 articulated vehicles, No 4034, is seen at Monkseaton. It would appear that the fine old station building was in the process of being dismantled. *Author*

Tynemouth

Then: 1951
The origins of the railway through Tynemouth lay with the Blyth & Tyne Railway. The line was electrified by the NER as part of its suburban scheme, with the first electric train reaching the station (from Monkseaton) on 21 June 1904. The station was extremely large and catered for both suburban and holiday traffic, Tynemouth being a popular destination for day trips to the coast.
Ian Allan Library (L&GRP 25560)

North Wylam

Then: 4 July 1953
This photograph shows the view looking east towards Newcastle. The line from Scotswood to Wylam, along the north bank of the Tyne, was authorised in 1871 and opened some five years later. The name Wylam should be familiar to all railway enthusiasts as the place where George Stephenson grew up. *C. D. Robinson*

Hexham

Then: September 1971
The first section of the Newcastle & Carlisle Railway to open, on 9 March 1835, was the section eastwards from Hexham to Blaydon. The station was eventually to become a junction for two branches: to Reedsmouth (opened in 1862) and to Allendale that opened later the same decade. The attractive station dates back to the 1830s. *Andrew Muckley*

Now: 11 June 1996
The northern parts of the Tyneside electrification scheme were converted to DMU operation in 1967. BR services over the line from West Monkseaton to Tynemouth and from Tynemouth to Heaton were withdrawn on 10 September 1979 and 11 August 1980 to allow for conversion to the Tyne & Wear Metro. Today you couldn't find a sharper contrast between the past and present than at Tynemouth. The Metro-Cammell-built vehicles, working now on only two through lines, are totally surrounded by the Victorian ironwork, which has been well restored in those parts of the station still in use. Unit No 4031 makes a brief stop in platform No 2. A station well worth a visit. *Author*

Now: 11 June 1996
The line through North Wylam lost its freight services on 1 January 1961 and passenger services followed on 11 March 1968. Wylam itself continues to be served by trains on the Newcastle-Carlisle route. Today the station site has been landscaped and the trackbed made into a walkway, which passes the cottage that was Stephenson's birthplace. *Author*

Now: 10 June 1996
Today the station is still extremely well maintained, with regular services to both Carlisle and Newcastle, although the lines to Reedsmouth and Allendale have long gone. Here Class 156 No 156444 is shown ready to depart with the 14.45 service to Sunderland. *Author*

Staward

*Then: c*1950
This was the last station before the terminus on the Allendale branch. The line lost its passenger services on 22 September 1930, although freight was to survive until 20 November 1950. Blaydon-allocated Class J21 0-6-0 No 65082 is shown at the station heading for Allendale. The locomotive was to outlast the branch by some five years, being withdrawn in 1955. *Neville Stead Collection*

Allendale

Then: 1930
The branch to Allendale, which left the main Newcastle & Carlisle Railway at Hexham, opened on 13 January 1868 for freight traffic and on 1 March 1869 for passenger services. A proposed extension was never constructed. Passenger services were withdrawn on 22 September 1930, the year in which this photograph was taken. The locomotive would appear to be a Class G5 0-4-4T. *Ian Allan Library (6328)*

Haydon Bridge

Then: 21 March 1965
The line westwards from Hexham to Haydon Bridge opened on 28 June 1836 and the station was the terminus of trains from Newcastle until the opening of the section from Blenkinsop Colliery, to the west, on 18 June 1838. Here an RCTS special from Leeds, headed by Class A1 4-6-2 No 60131 *Osprey*, makes an unscheduled stop *en route* to Carlisle due to the presence of sheep on the line. No 60131 was to be withdrawn six months later. *Author*

Now: 10 June 1996
Today the view from the bridge is very restricted, but the station house, which is occupied, is just visible through the trees and bushes. *Author*

Now: 10 June 1996
Although passenger services over the branch were withdrawn on 22 September 1930, freight continued to operate for a further 20 years until 20 November 1950. The station is now a fine residence and the area formerly occupied by the tracks has been made into an extremely well-kept caravan site. Apart from the walls around the loading bays, there was little to remind you that this was once a branch line terminus, except for the station building itself. *Author*

Now: 10 June 1996
Although there has been some rationalisation of the old station buildings and the construction of a bus stop-type shelter, Haydon Bridge remains open. Here a Strathclyde PTE-liveried Class 156, No 156501, halts with a service from Newcastle to Stranraer. *Author*

Haltwhistle

Then: August 1951
Haltwhistle, as the station board makes clear, was where passengers from Alston changed for trains to Newcastle and Carlisle. The 13-mile-long branch to the Cumbrian market town of Alston opened in 1852; the route included some nine viaducts and several severe gradients. On the date of this photograph 'G5' class 0-4-4T No 67315 was working the branch service. *Ian Allan Library (K1220)*

Now: 10 June 1996
Haltwhistle station remains open, although the branch to Alston has closed and the track has been lifted from this platform. Services over the Alston line were withdrawn from 3 May 1976, after the completion of a supposed all-weather road had made the railway apparently redundant. The signalbox, located just behind the photographer, still stands, but is now unused, the signalman operating from the cabin to the right of the station building. A regular hourly service still operates in both directions over the main line. *Author*

Alston

Then: Undated
The 13-mile branch line from Haltwhistle to Alston opened on 17 November 1852. At over 900ft, Alston is one of the highest market towns in England, and has a population of some 2,000. Class G5 0-4-4T No 67315 was working the passenger service in this photograph taken in the mid-1950s, whilst 'J39' 0-6-0 No 64842 was resting in the little engine shed. The shed at Alston was a sub-shed to that at Blaydon. *Neville Stead Collection*

Now: 10 June 1996
Although the line closed in May 1976, rails still exist at Alston, as the station is now the headquarters of the narrow gauge South Tynedale Railway. Originally a preservation group was established to restore the whole line to the standard gauge, but the costs proved prohibitive. With help from the English Tourist Board and from the local authorities, a 2ft 0in gauge line was started in 1980, with the first train running in 1983. An extension as far as Gilderdale was opened in 1987. The signalbox seen in the background was originally at Ainderby on the Northallerton-Hawes line. *Author*

Brampton Junction

Then: 1930
Towards the western end of the Newcastle & Carlisle line is Brampton Junction, which is situated on the section of the route, between Carlisle and Greenhead, that opened on 19 July 1836. This was not, in fact, the oldest railway serving Brampton, as a wagonway linking Brampton with Lambley was opened in 1799. Part of this wagonway was converted to form the Brampton Junction-Brampton Town branch, whilst the section south to Lambley (where after 1852 it formed a junction with the Alston branch) remained a mineral line, passing eventually to National Coal Board ownership. The branch to Brampton Town lost its passenger services even before the date of this photograph, on 31 December 1923. This view looking east shows the line of the branch towards Lambley. *Ian Allan Library (6263)*

Now: 10 June 1996
The mineral line towards Lambley closed in March 1953 and few traces of it survive here. The Brampton Town branch lost its freight services on 5 July 1965. The station at Brampton Junction remains open, although this Class 156 No 156469, on the 12.35 Carlisle-Newcastle service, is not scheduled to call at it. Note that whilst the signalbox still stands, it is derelict and the remaining semaphore signals are controlled by the next box along the line. *Author*

Newbiggin by the Sea

Then: June 1956
The branch to Newbiggin was authorised in 1867 by the Blyth & Tyne Railway; the B&T became part of the NER in 1874. The line ran through Ashington, famous for its industrial network, to North Seaton and Bedlington. Here Heaton-allocated Class V3 2-6-2T No 67651 is shown ready to leave with a train for Newcastle.
Ian Allan Library (K3037)

Now: 11 June 1996
All services, both passenger and freight, were withdrawn from the Newbiggin branch on 2 November 1964. By that date No 67651 had also been taken out of service; it was withdrawn six months prior to the line's closure. The railway site is now a pleasant grassed area with no buildings. Judging by the number of houses that exist a few hundred yards beyond the former station, I am sure that if the line still operated today it would be well patronised. *Author*

Alnmouth

Then: 29 December 1962
A very dirty Gateshead-allocated 'A4' Pacific No 60001 *Sir Ronald Matthews* enters the station with a northbound service, with the small goods yard in the background. It was obviously a terrible day, as the sea cannot be seen in the background. Alnmouth was the junction for the branch to Alnwick. *M. Dunnett*

Now: 10 June 1996
The branch to Alnwick closed in 1968, but the station at Alnmouth survives today and, although the goods shed has been demolished, a few sidings remain for PW equipment. The down slow line has also disappeared. The 08.00 King's Cross-Edinburgh service rushes past, headed by Class 91 No 91028 *Guide Dog*. The station is actually in the village of Hipsburn, a short distance from Alnmouth itself. *Author*

Alnwick

Then: 21 May 1966
The very impressive station at Alnwick was built in the late 1880s to the design of William Bell and was similar, albeit smaller, to that which Bell designed at Darlington. The branch from Alnmouth to Alnwick opened in August 1850. The construction of the new station resulted from the opening of the Alnwick-Coldstream line, in 1887; passenger services over the route were withdrawn on 22 September 1930 and the final freight workings occurred in 1953, some five years after the line had been breached by serious flooding. Thompson-designed 'K1' 2-6-0s were often the motive power in the latter days of the line and here No 62050 is seen leaving for Alnmouth with a painted '10D' shed plate (which was Plodder Lane!). *Author*

Wooperton

Then: 1950
This station was situated on the line between Alnwick and Coldstream, about 15³⁄₄ miles from Alnwick. The route opened for freight services on 2 May 1887 and to passenger services on 5 September. Passenger services were withdrawn on 22 September, but at the time of this photograph, freight services were still operated.
Ian Allan Library (L&GRP 24674)

Now: 10 June 1996
The passenger services over the Alnwick branch were withdrawn on 29 January 1968, with freight being withdrawn from the line on 7 October the same year. The station building still stands, although, as can be seen, it is now used by a storage and haulage company. *Author*

Now: 11 June 1996
The section of line between Ilderton and Wooler was closed completely following flood damage in 1948, but the remaining sections of the line — south from Ilderton, via Wooperton, to Alnwick and north from Ilderton — retained freight services until 2 March 1953 and 29 March 1965 respectively. It was not possible to take the picture from the same spot, so I have taken this photograph looking in the opposite direction from the bridge shown in the 'Then' photograph in order to illustrate that a fine house has been constructed from the old station. The trackbed and yard are now occupied by a large timber company. *Author*

Ilderton

Then: 1950
The next station along the line from Wooperton to Coldstream was that at Ilderton. This was, by the date of this photograph, the terminus of the freight-only route from Alnwick, the line beyond to Wooler having closed completely in 1948. *Ian Allan Library (L&GRP 24673)*

Now: 11 June 1996
Given the lack of freight activity in the 'Then' photograph, it will come as little surprise that freight services over the truncated route were withdrawn in 1953. This picture has been included because the site has been developed into a restaurant, which is full of railway interest, plenty of photographs and railwayana. Outside is an ex-Western Region camping coach, No W334 built at Swindon in 1951. If you are in the area, it is well worth a visit. *Author*

Kirknewton

Then: 14 April 1963
Passenger services over the line from Alnwick to Coldstream had long been withdrawn when this special, headed by Ivatt 2-6-0 No 46474, visited the truncated remains of the line. The line had been severed south of Ilderton in 1948 by heavy flooding. *W. S. Sellar*

Now: 11 June 1996
The freight services between Coldstream and Wooler were withdrawn on 29 March 1965. Although the track is long gone from this location, there is still a great deal to remind you that this was once a station including (*inset*) this ornate gateway. *Author (both)*

Mindrum

Then: 1950
The last station on the line from Alnwick before reaching the junction at Coldstream was Mindrum. The stations on this line were particularly impressive, especially considering the small communities that they were designed to serve. *Ian Allan Library (L&GRP 24665)*

Now: 11 June 1996
I have included a number of photographs from this attractive line because of the superb restorations visible. As with the rest of the line between Coldstream and Wooler, freight services through the station were withdrawn on 29 March 1965. The station at Mindrum is now a superb residence with well-landscaped gardens. The old goods shed has been utilised by the house's owner for his business. *Author*

Coldstream

Then: 1 June 1962
Coldstream was the junction where the line from Alnwick, which had opened in 1887, met the line from Tweedmouth to Roxburgh and Kelso. This route, which was NER owned as far as Sprouston Junction, just over the border in Roxburghshire, opened on 27 July 1849. This delightful branch line photograph shows Ivatt 2-6-0 No 46482 shunting wagons prior to returning to Kelso. Beyong Sprouston Junction the line was owned by the North British Railway. Even by the date of this photograph the railway facilities at Coldstream had been reduced with the closure of the line south to Wooler in 1953. *M. Mensing*

Now: 11 June 1996
The line was closed completely on 29 March 1965 and, as can be seen, the station has not survived and the site has been redeveloped. I am grateful to the local gentleman who told me where to stand. *Author*

List of Locations